To Dean Ra
and the
Judith Herb College of Education

Enjoy a little Toledo
history That was made
possible by Education!

Tom Brady

MW00823761

Impact of Owens-Illinois on the World

Business Enterprises and Companies
Founded by or directed by former Owens-Illinois Employees

By Dr. Tom Brady
Vice President, Plastics Technology
Owens-Illinois, Inc. (O-I) 1972-1985
Founder and Chairman Emeritus
Plastic Technologies, Inc. (PTI) 1985-2021

Copyright © 2021 by Thomas Brady
All rights reserved
ISBN 978-1-66782-131-3
Printed by BookBaby
7905 N. Crescent Blvd. Pennsauken, NJ 08110
1-877-961-6878
info@bookbaby.com

Direct any comments or questions or requests for an electronic copy of this book to: drtombrady1944@gmail.com
Bound copies of this book can be purchased from Amazon or from any bookstore

Acknowledgements

A history, by definition, is a collection of memories, analyzed and reduced to meaningful conclusions. This summary of the 29 employees who left Owens-Illinois, Inc. (O-I) from 1960 to 1990 to start or run other companies is, however, as much a collection of the memories of those who helped create that history, as it is of my own memories.

Unfortunately, many of those who did leave O-I to create or to run companies are no longer with us but, in addition to the research I have done to fill in some of the missing stories, I have been fortunate to have several of those former O-I employees help me by writing or editing their own stories, including in alphabetical order, Mike Charchol, Mike Horner, Saleh Jabarin, Kim Klewer, Randall Litten, Paul Rothschild, Keith Sponseller (son of Harold Sponseller), Dennis Sturgil, Mike Wilhelm (son of Don Wilhelm), and Paul Young, as well as several colleagues of those former O-I employees, including David Levison and Jerry Schermerhorn.

Most importantly, I owe this entire history to my wife and best friend, Betsy Brady, who not only enthusiastically encouraged and supported me in my own career at O-I and after I left O-I in 1985, but who also encouraged and supported my effort to document the history of PTI and the histories of those former O-I employees who left O-I and who have collectively made a huge impact on the world.

In addition to this book which I am dedicating to all my former O-I colleagues, I have also written and published two additional, but related historical books, including "The History of the PET Bottle," and "The Story of PTI," which provide more detail about my career in the packaging industry.

Table of Contents

Owens-Illinois, Inc.

from www.CompanyHistories.com

Website: https://www.company-histories.com/Owens-Illinois-Inc-Company-History.html#

Statistics:

Public Company
Incorporated: 1907 as The Owens Bottle Machine Corporation
Employees: 32,400 (1997)
Sales: $4.66 billion (1997)
Stock Exchange: New York
Ticker Symbol: OI

Company Overview (1997)

Owens-Illinois is one of the world's leading manufacturers of packaging products. It is the largest manufacturer of glass containers in North America, South America, and India, and the second largest in Europe. Approximately one of every two glass containers made worldwide is made by Owens-Illinois, its affiliates, or its licensees. The company's plastics group manufactures a wide variety of plastic packaging items including containers, closures, trigger sprayers, finger pumps, prescription containers, labels, and multipack carriers for beverage containers. Owens-Illinois is the leader in technology, the high-productivity, low-cost producer, and the leading supplier in almost all of the markets it serves.

Company History (1997)

Owens-Illinois, Inc. is one of the largest manufacturers of glass containers and plastic packaging in the world. About half of the glass containers made worldwide are made by Owens-Illinois. It holds the top position in glass containers in the United States, North America, South America, Australia, New Zealand, and India, and the number two position in Europe (behind Compagnie de Saint-Gobain).

In 1997, 71 of overall sales stemmed from glass. The remaining revenue was generated from the company's plastics group, which is a leading worldwide maker of plastics packaging, including containers, closures, prescription containers, labels, and multipack carriers for beverage bottles. With 144 manufacturing plants in 24 countries, an increasingly global Owens-Illinois generates about 37 percent of sales outside the United States.

Early History

The Toledo-based company was incorporated in Ohio in 1907 as The Owens Bottle Machine Corporation, the successor to a New Jersey firm of the same name founded in 1903. It took the name Owens-Illinois Glass Company following the 1929 merger of Owens Bottle and the Illinois Glass Company of Alton, Illinois, a small manufacturer of glass products for the drug and medical fields. Like most can and bottle making companies, Owens-Illinois weathered the years of the Great Depression without a production slowdown. Throughout the 20th century the container industry as a whole proved itself to be almost unaffected by dramatic swings in the economy.

In 1935 Owens-Illinois acquired the Libbey-Glass Company and entered the consumer tableware field. The Libbey division was responsible for making tumblers, glass pitchers, dishes, and bowls.

Soon afterward, Owens began conducting experiments with glass fibers, learning that one of its chief competitors, Corning Glass, was doing similar research. The two firms agreed to cooperate and formed Owens-Corning Fiberglass in 1938. Development of marketable fiberglass products quickly followed. Corning and Owens, with their virtual monopoly on fiberglass technology, profited greatly. Following a 1949 antitrust ruling that barred Corning and Owens from controlling Owens-Corning, the joint venture was taken public in 1952, with shares distributed, one-third each, to Owens, Corning, and the public. Subsequently, both Owens-Illinois and Corning Glass sold their shares in Owens-Corning.

During the period immediately following World War II, Owens-Illinois remained primarily a glassmaker, its few deviations from the bottle business being limited to those areas on the immediate periphery of glass containers.

This was all soon to change, however. A number of antitrust rulings in the late 1940s restricted companies such as Owens-Illinois from increasing market share through wholesale acquisitions of subsidiaries in their respective industries. Growth, it seemed, would have to come from fields outside glass.

Meanwhile, from 1948 through 1958, Owens-Illinois made asbestos pipe and boiler insulation under the brand Kaylo. Though it sold this fairly small business to Owens-Corning in 1958, the company's production of an asbestos-laden product would result in extended litigation in the 1980s and 1990s.

Diversification in the 1950s and 1960s

The first significant diversification move came in 1956 when Owens purchased the National Container Corporation, America's third largest box maker at the time. The move into forest products, though gradual, was as predictable as it was necessary.

It made good economic sense to make a forest products company part of the Owens-Illinois holdings. Not only was the parent firm supplied cardboard boxes at reduced rates, but the paper and pulp sector turned profits of its own.

In the 1950s Owens-Illinois took another step outside the glass container field, into a promising new area, plastic containers. The company had for some time made plastic caps and closures, but up until the mid-1950s the technology for making plastic containers was not available. This changed very quickly.

Most popular at that time was the plastic squeeze-bottle which could be used as a container for prepared mustard and other sauces. Owens-Illinois, however, directed its energy toward semirigid plastic containers, and this strategy was successful. In 1958 Owens-Illinois persuaded a number of large bleach and laundry detergent companies to switch to the new bottles. The plastic bottles were immediately popular with consumers and continued to gain favor during succeeding decades. Each year plastic containers claimed a more substantial share of counter space in American supermarkets.

Despite the important advances in paper and plastics, the company was still very much committed to glass manufacturing.

The 1960s were years of tremendous growth in both can and bottle manufacturing. Although the two industries were rivals for the growing consumer beverage market, there was enough soft beverage and beer business for all the container companies.

The intense competition was for the lion's share, and the initial demand for the new pop-top can relegated glass containers to a distant second place.

Then the ever-bothersome returnable bottle, with its thick glass and mandatory deposit, gave way to the lighter "one-way" bottle. The new construction ushered in a renaissance for the glass industry, allowing it to challenge the can industry more effectively. Since the one-way bottle was not returned for refilling it could be made of thinner glass. This meant production cost and production time were reduced, thereby increasing profit margins. Although many industry analysts thought the glass beverage container was destined to failure in the early 1960s it did not surrender its market share to the pull-tab can; bottle sales tripled that decade.

Still, Owens-Illinois was aware that diversification efforts would have to be accelerated if growth was to continue. The burgeoning of the beverage market during the 1960s was not to be repeated, and expansion in glass manufacturing slowed considerably.

The company involved itself in such far-removed fields as sugar cane farming in the Bahamas and phosphate rock mining in Florida. During the late 1960s Lily Tulip Cups, maker of everything from wax-lined milk cartons to disposable cups, was acquired. Moves such as these prompted Owens-Illinois to drop the word "glass" from its corporate name, becoming Owens-Illinois, Inc.

O-I's Toledo Headquarters Over the Years
This story is courtesy of The Toledo Blade and Homer Brickey, published on Feb 3, 2005

The first five sites for offices of Toledo's second-largest corporation - and the world's largest glass-container maker - have some things in common.

All were in new or relatively new buildings. For the most part, they were in the finest office quarters Toledo had to offer at the time. All are still standing. And four of the five are in a tight grouping, within a golf shot of each other, in downtown Toledo.

In September 1903, the Owens Bottle Machine Co., O-I's predecessor, began selling automated bottle-making machinery perfected by Michael J. Owens.

Its choice of headquarters location was a natural one, offices in the Spitzer Building at Madison Avenue and Huron Street downtown, billed as Toledo's first "skyscraper" at 10 stories high. The Spitzer Building, completed in 1896, was a commercial hub, and an added attraction was the Toledo Stock Exchange, formed just five months before the Owens firm.

But in 1906, a more modern building opened across the street. It was the 17-story Nicholas Building, tallest in Ohio at the time. It was a big lure for the budding Owens firm, which moved there in 1908. Years later, the Nicholas building was renamed the National Bank Building and is now known as Fifth Third Center.

The Owens company prospered. By 1916, the New York Stock exchange listed its shares, and by 1919 it was called Owens Bottle Co.

Owens remained in the Nicholas Building 20 years. In 1928, the company moved to its new headquarters at 965 Wall St., next to the first Owens Bottle factory. Wall is a short industrial street off Detroit Avenue midway between Monroe Street and Central Avenue.

A 1929 event created a glass giant: Owens Bottle merged with Illinois Glass Co., of Alton, Ill., and the headquarters of the new Owens-Illinois Glass Co. remained in Toledo.

Although the Depression ruined many companies, including banks, it created opportunities for O-I.

Within a few years after the merger, the bottle business was booming, thanks largely to the repeal of Prohibition, and O-I steadily bought out less fortunate glass companies. By 1935, O-I had 600 executives and office workers.

The Depression created another bit of serendipity for O-I - readily available, attractive space in the 29-story Ohio Bank Building at Madison Avenue and St. Clair Street. Ohio Savings Bank & Trust Co., which owned the building, failed, and at one point the 368-foot structure (tallest in Ohio at the time) was half vacant.

In mid-1935, O-I leased seven floors. Soon, it was the main tenant, and in 1945 it acquired the structure and added the lighted O-I atop the building a decade later.

O-I's former headquarters on Wall Street were Toledo's relief offices late in the Depression. From 1939 to 1976, the building was an Ohio National Guard armory, and in the 1980s it was the city's fire department engine-repair garage. In recent years, it has been used as a warehouse by a private business.

During the 46 years O-I occupied the building at Madison and St. Clair, the firm became a multinational manufacturer and was chosen as one of the prestigious 30 companies on the Dow Jones industrial average. O-I moved out in 1981, and the structure is now known as the National City Bank Building.

O-I had grown tremendously by the 1970s, and it was a multibillion-dollar firm looking for a new headquarters.

Its options included building next to its existing headquarters, building on its Perrysburg land, or moving to swank quarters in a city like Atlanta. O-I chose to build a 32-story, $100 million steel-and-glass skyscraper along the Maumee riverfront.

It was called One SeaGate but was also known as the O-I World Headquarters, largely at the urging of the late Edwin D. Dodd, longtime CEO, and a champion of downtown Toledo. O-I relocated 2,000 employees into the building.

After the takeover by KKR in 1987 and then after a major downsizing,

going public again, and selling off most operations except for glass containers, O-I built its most recent headquarters in Levis Park located in Perrysburg OH and moved its remaining nearly 600 employees to the Perrysburg business park.

Modernizing Facilities in the 1970s

As beverage sales leveled off in the 1970s, the container industry found itself in the midst of a worldwide recession. Many large can and bottle customers, which included large breweries and soft drink companies, began manufacturing their own containers.

Many can and bottle manufacturers had unwisely increased the size of their container-producing facilities and were now confronted with overcapacity, an unwieldy workforce, and tumbling prices. The problem was particularly acute in bottle manufacturing where production was more labor-intensive.

Owens-Illinois attempted to solve this problem through technology, investing in new industrial equipment that could make 20 bottles in the time it used to take to make six, and therefore cutting labor costs. Also, the company dedicated more factory space, often entire plants, to single product lines for one customer. However, these were stop-gap measures and did not solve the overall problem. Wholesale modernization was necessary.

As Owens-Illinois entered the 1980s its production costs advantage, once the envy of the industry, had been eroded. While the company developed revolutionary new container machinery, it allowed the majority of its conventional glass plants to deteriorate. Edwin D. Dodd, the company's chief executive officer, divested marginal interests, which were draining resources and performing poorly, and supervised a $911 million four-year plant modernization program.

More importantly, the company's attitude toward its own industry changed, particularly regarding bottle manufacturing. Historically a large volume dealer concerned with maintaining its huge market share, Owens-Illinois began to emphasize profit margins rather than its share of the bottle manufacturing market. Unprofitable plants, even relatively new ones, were closed or sold; production of the two-way returnable bottle was discontinued in favor of the exclusive manufacture of the "one-way" bottle; and the minimum order level was raised while the customer base was reduced to a number of large-volume, blue-chip customers. The results of this policy were impressive.

Capacity was reduced by 24 percent and the workforce was cut by 30 percent. Owens-Illinois was again able to reclaim its productive edge over competitors.

Owens-Illinois' regard for the natural environment drew the attention and praise of consumer advocate Ralph Nader. In his 1971 study on water pollution, Nader cited Owens-Illinois as the industrial company with the best record on environmental issues. The compliment was well-deserved. The company's glass factories were among the safest and cleanest in the business; it led the industry in recycling; and it advocated a national system of resource recovery to deal with the mounting solid waste problem.

Owens-Illinois' environmental policies came about largely through the work of a former chief executive officer, Raymond Mulford, who died in 1973. He had encouraged community participation on behalf of his staff and factory workers and devoted nearly half of his time in later years to social and environmental programs. Most company plants were located in small towns, and Mulford insisted they be an asset, not a liability, to the community.

This meant confronting the issue of pollution control long before it was a national concern.

By the early 1980s the modernized Owens-Illinois company was the most formidable member of the glass container industry. It outproduced its competitors by 33 percent. Yet, to increase profit margins and efficiency, company operations were streamlined. The company invested heavily in research and developed production methods that reduced the labor content of a finished glass product from 40 percent to 20 percent. A total of 48 plants were closed and 17,000 workers laid off. The jobs of 46,000 other employees, however, were saved.

Many of Owens-Illinois's rivals did not spend the money necessary to compete. Thatcher Glass, once number two in the industry, went bankrupt in 1981, its failure the product of a poorly executed leveraged buyout and an unwillingness to rebuild old furnaces and install new technology.

Other manufacturers, such as Anchor-Hocking and Glass Containers Corporation, found themselves in similar predicaments.

Robert Lanigan, the CEO of Owens-Illinois during the 1980s, emphasized the manufacture of plastic bottles and the increasingly popular plastic-shield glass bottle. He also continued the diversification program and acquired two nursing home chains and the Alliance Mortgage Company, a mortgage banking concern. Owens-Illinois' policies were aimed at reducing the company's vulnerability to a takeover. Since the container industry was mature and growing slowly, return on stockholder's equity was, in the mid-1980s, less than 10%. Thus, Owens-Illinois' stock price was well below book value; at the same time, it had an attractive annual cash flow of $300 million.

KKR Leveraged Buyout in 1987

In the end, Lanigan's efforts could not stave off a takeover. On December 11, 1986, Kohlberg Kravis Roberts & Company (KKR), a holding company specializing in taking firms private, offered to purchase Owens-Illinois for $55 per share. Owens-Illinois refused the offer and threatened to initiate a reorganization, including the sale of over $1 billion in assets, in order to protect the company from subsequent takeover attempts. KKR responded by raising its bid to $60 per share. When investment houses acting on behalf of Owens-Illinois failed to find buyers willing to outbid KKR, Owens-Illinois officials were forced to negotiate.

In mid-February 1987, Owens-Illinois announced that it had agreed to be acquired by a KKR subsidiary, the Oil Acquisition Corporation, for $60.50 per share, or about $3.6 billion. In order to finance the leveraged buyout a number of banks agreed to extend a short-term, or "bridge," loan of $600 million to KKR, to be paid back over 18 months through an issue of high-yield bonds.

KKR had first established a relationship with Owens-Illinois in 1981, when it purchased cupmaker Lily Tulip from Owens-Illinois. While some members of the Owens-Illinois board opposed the takeover (and opposed becoming a private company), it was generally agreed that the short-term interests of the stockholders were served.

Over the next few years KKR-led Owens-Illinois divested several noncore operations, in part to pay down the hefty $4.4 billion debt on the company books following the LBO and in part because a prime reason to diversify--fending off raiders--was now moot. In addition to jettisoning the forest products and mortgage banking units, Owens-Illinois sold its healthcare businesses in 1991 for $369 million.

Meanwhile, the company moved to significantly bolster its share of the U.S. glass container market through a $750 million 1987 acquisition of Jacksonville, Florida-based Brockway Inc. The merger of two of the three largest U.S. glass container makers was initially blocked by the U.S. Federal Trade Commission (FTC), which contended that the combination would create a company with too much control of the market, with a 38 percent share. Owens-Illinois took its case to federal court, winning an appeal in 1988. The following year, however, an FTC administrative law judge ruled that the company should be forced to sell Brockway, leading to another Owens-Illinois appeal. Finally, in March 1992 the chairman of the FTC overturned the earlier ruling, allowing the acquisition to stand.

Somewhat ironically, in December 1991 a federal jury had found that Owens-Illinois and Brockway (along with Dart Industries Inc.) had conspired to fix prices on glass containers in the 1970s and 1980s. A settlement on the damages was soon reached out of court, with the terms not disclosed.

Public Again in 1991

In December 1991 KKR took Owens-Illinois public once again, through an initial public offering (IPO) that raised about $1.3 billion. The proceeds were used to further pay down debt, which by 1993 stood at $2.5 billion. KKR maintained a stake of about 26 percent through the late 1990s.

Over the next several years after the IPO, Owens-Illinois concentrated on building up its core glass container and plastic packaging operations. Much of the growth would come in the form of acquisitions-- particularly overseas--but the company also spent more than $1.5 billion in capital expenditures from 1993 through 1997 to improve productivity and increase capacity of existing facilities.

The company's involvement in the plastics industry also expanded, evolving into a plastics group producing containers, closures, prescription containers, labels, and multipack carriers for beverage bottles. The 1992 acquisition of Specialty Packaging Products, Inc. brought Owens-Illinois a leading U.S. manufacturer of trigger sprayers and finger pumps, with annual sales of $100 million.

During the mid-1990s the company continued to affirm its concentration on glass containers and plastic packaging through several strategic divestments. In 1994 and 1995 it sold off its specialty glass segment.

Also, in 1994 Libbey Glass was spun off, becoming the publicly traded Libbey Inc. Owens-Illinois in December 1993 sold 51 percent of specialty packaging and laboratory equipment maker Kimble Glass Inc. to Gerresheimer Glas AG. It sold the remaining 49 percent stake to Gerresheimer in March 1997.

Mid-1990s Global Expansion

A serious international presence began in 1993 with an expansion of South American operations, leading to the company's capture of the number one position in glass containers on that continent. Another top position, in India, was gained in 1994 through the acquisition of glass container maker Ballarpur Industries. Three years later Owens-Illinois spent about $586 million for AVIR S.p.A., the largest manufacturer of glass containers in Italy. By this time the company also held leading positions in this segment in the United Kingdom, Poland, Hungary, Finland, Estonia, and had gained the number two position overall in Europe.

Back home, Owens-Illinois paid about $125 million in February 1997 to acquire the glass container assets of Anchor Glass Container Corporation, in the process increasing its share of the U.S. market to more than 40 percent. Also, during 1997 the company completed a major refinancing, which included the retirement of about $1.9 billion in high-cost debt.

In April 1998 Owens-Illinois paid $3.6 billion in cash for the worldwide glass and plastics packaging businesses of BTR plc of the United Kingdom, in the largest acquisition in company history. Added thereby to the Owens-Illinois empire was ACI Glass Packaging, the only maker of glass containers in Australia and New Zealand, with additional operations in China and Indonesia; and U.S.-based Continental PET Technologies, a leading supplier of plastic food and drink containers in the United States, Australia, New Zealand, the United Kingdom, the Netherlands, and Brazil, China, Hungary, Mexico, and Saudi Arabia.

The Commission of the European Communities approved the purchase but with the stipulation that Owens-Illinois sell BTR's glass container operations in the United Kingdom, known as Rockware Glass.

Throughout the 1990s the company had to contend with ongoing asbestos litigation stemming from its Kaylo insulation business of 1948--58. By the end of 1997 Owens-Illinois had settled claims involving about 210,000 claimants, with an average payment per claim of $4,200. The company had itself sued more than two dozen insurance companies who had refused to cover these claims. By 1997 Owens-Illinois had reached settlements with a number of these insurers, resulting in about $308.4 million in coverage for the company. It expected to receive substantial additional payments as the remaining suits reached settlements. Owens-Illinois was still a named defendant in asbestos claims involving about 14,000 claimants by the end of 1997, and new claims were filed each year, although the number was steadily decreasing.

Even prior to the acquisition of BTR's packaging units, Owens-Illinois had more than doubled its sales outside the United States. In 1997 non-U.S. revenue accounted for 37 percent of overall company revenue, which had reached a record $4.66 billion. With its concentration on the core areas of glass containers and plastic packaging and with its aggressive program of international expansion, Owens-Illinois appeared to have in place a solid plan for 21st-century growth.

Principal Subsidiaries:

Owens-Illinois Group, Inc.; OI Health Care Holding Corp.; OI General Finance Inc.; OI Closure FTS Inc.; OI Plastic Products FTS Inc.; Owens-Illinois Prescription Products Inc.; Owens-Brockway Plastic Products Inc.; Owens-Illinois Labels Inc.; Owens-Brockway Packaging, Inc.; OI Ione STS Inc.; Owens-Brockway Glass Container Inc. The company also lists subsidiaries in the following countries: Bolivia, Brazil, Bermuda, China, Colombia, Czech Republic, Ecuador, Estonia, Finland, Hungary, India, Italy, Mexico, the Netherlands, Peru, Poland, Spain, Thailand, the United Kingdom, and Venezuela.

Further Reading:

Henderson, Angelo B., "Owens-Illinois Agrees to Acquire Glass, Plastic Line of BTR for $3.6 Billion," *Wall Street Journal,* March 2, 1998, pp. A13.

Norman, James R., "Smart Timing," *Forbes,* November 25, 1991, pp. 170+.

Willoughby, Jack, "Owens-Illinois: Wishful Recap," *Financial World,* May 14, 1991, pp.

Source: *International Directory of Company Histories*, Vol. 26. St. James Press, 1999.

A Contemporary History of Owens-Illinois
By Mr. Kim Klewer, former Owens-Illinois Corporate Security Specialist

<u>One Seagate</u> (Mid 1970's): The vision of O-I Chairman of the Board, Ed Dodd, and other senior O-I management members was not simply that O-I was going to build a new downtown Toledo high-rise headquarters building. Rather, Mr. Dodd's vision was that One Seagate would serve to revitalize a struggling downtown and become the catalyst to restore downtown as a destination, particularly along the riverfront and by creating the now prominent (1975) Promenade Park.

Downtown Toledo in the mid/late-1970s was in desperate need of revitalization. Suburban malls had killed downtown shopping, movie theaters were being torn down, hotels were struggling, corporations were relocating to the suburbs, and there was an ever-diminishing downtown nightlife after 5:00, with ever increasing vacant buildings and vacant land.

O-I's and Ed Dodd's vision included a vibrant riverfront park, a riverfront hotel, a marina, an ice rink, shopping, restaurants, and something that would be brand new to Toledo, underground and overhead pedestrian connectors from new parking garages that would connect downtown workers and visitors with restaurants, shopping, and downtown events. This was the vision of O-I and particularly of Ed Dodd.

It should also be noted that Ed Dodd had a visionary partner, George Haigh, who at the time was president of the Toledo Trust Company (eventually Trust Corp, then Society Corp, and now KeyCorp), the leading Downtown Toledo bank. Together, Ed Dodd and George Haigh led the transformation of Toledo's riverfront, which eventually led to many downtown improvements.

It is also worth noting that in 1981 when O-I moved into their new One Seagate headquarters, O-I occupied the entire 28 floors of the building, except for two floors which were leased to O-I's outside accounting firm, Arthur Young, Inc.

<u>Levis Development Park</u> (known today as Levis Commons): In the 1960's O-I purchased about 400 acres on US route 25, contiguous to the planned construction of I-475 in Perrysburg Township.

With O-I's 1960's growth and diversification, J. Preston Levis, O-I Chairman (1950 – 1968) envisioned that all Toledo area O-I facilities would be located at one site and that O-I would pioneer the almost unheard of concept of an upscale office/industrial park with mixed use of R&D facilities, manufacturing plants, a world headquarters office building, access to rail and interstate transportation, not to mention park-like amenities for employees and a research and development atmosphere that would inspire creativity and innovation, all in one location.

14

Under J P Levis' oversight, by 1968 a four-lane entry boulevard off US RT 25 was constructed with a partial road system that connected four newly constructed O-I facilities at the rear of Levis Park. Levis Park's infrastructure was cutting-edge for the times and included all underground utilities, curbed roads with sewers, a separate electric power sub-station as well as natural gas and telephone sub-stations, and fire sprinklers in all the buildings were served by a massive central diesel fire pump and a site-wide lawn sprinkler system. All this infrastructure was necessary since the original master plan called for construction of 19 facilities including a new O-I world headquarters building at the end of the entry boulevard.

Levis Park's 1968 four facilities were quite diverse and included Bldg. 25, the Ink & Die facility which produced ink and printed all O-I forms, Bldg 29, the Solder Glass plant, later to be converted to an aluminum can plant, and then to a plastics R&D facility, Bldg 30, the Digivue facility which housed O-I's flatscreen R&D operation, and Bldg 13 which housed O-I's new deposable, wide mouth, glass beverage container manufacturing operation and which was shuttered after just 4 years. Bldg 13 now contains the Schutz Container Systems company.

J P Levis who was also credited with guiding O-I's expansion into plastics and paper products retired in 1968 and died in 1973. With him also died the concept of O-I's Levis Development Park. New corporate leadership shifted the focus of O-I to remain an important Downtown Toledo-based company. Consequently, Levis Development Park remained stagnant until the year 2000 when O-I sold about 300 of the unused acres or 75% of Levis Park to Dillin Development Corporation which has since developed and constructed what is known today as Levis Commons. Ironically, part of J P Levis' vision came true in 2006, when O-I built a new world headquarters building at the Levis Commons property and as O-I vacated their One Seagate World Headquarters in downtown Toledo.

It is also worth noting that J P Levis was the last founding family member from the Illinois Glass Company (est.1873 by Edward Levis) to serve as O-I's Chairman.

Since its inception in 1929 and for 77 years, Owens-Illinois, Inc. had been headquartered in downtown Toledo and more than one person over the years has told me that the O-I management model was taught and used as a business model in Harvard's MBA graduate studies back in the DOW 30 era.

Plastic Technologies, Inc. (PTI)
Founder - Dr. Tom Brady
Former VP of Plastics Technology at O-I

PTI Website: https://www.plastictechnologies.com/
Interview with Tom Brady: https://www.plastictechnologies.com/tom-brady/
Tom Brady personal information: https://www.linkedin.com/in/dr-tom-brady-002a172/

 **PTI** was founded in 1985 by Thomas E. Brady, PhD, who previously served as the VP and Director of Plastics Technology for Owens-Illinois Inc., where he helped lead the development of PET bottle technology from 1971 to 1984. Because of these innovations, Brady was approached by Coca-Cola to lead a number of projects, which resulted in the establishment of an independent company—Plastic Technologies, Inc.

Owens-Illinois (O-I) employees who also eventually transitioned to **PTI** and who helped create the other 5 **PTI** companies formed over **PTI's** 35-year history include Duane Nugent, Al Uhlig, Jim Berry, Bob Deardurff, Scott Steele, Don Hayward, Frank Semersky, Jack Ritchie, Dennis Balduff, Oliver Brownridge, and Frank Schloss.

PTI - The Beginning

Teaming Up with Coca-Cola

Coca-Cola put **PTI** on the map, signing Brady as the sole PET expert. He became the manager of project development efforts for converting the Coca-Cola glass bottle shape into plastic in order to retain the company's iconic brand image. Contractual funding provided credibility for **PTI** to quickly identify additional customers, and to attract and hire a small, but highly experienced staff.

Gaining Traction and Initial Growth

As **PTI** became immersed in important package development programs for several other large customers, it quickly established a reputation as a high-quality PET R&D and technical support resource.

PTI became a Trusted Innovation Partner for Brands

Over time, **PTI** developed relationships with other high-profile brands, self-manufacturers, resin suppliers, machinery builders and converters. **PTI** learned how to work with competitive customers and was recognized for excellence in protecting customer intellectual property and confidentiality.

PTI Created a Reputation for Sustainable Packaging Innovation

PTI is recognized as the sustainable plastic packaging company and premier PET technical development and support resource in the industry, with offices and labs in the US, Switzerland and India. The company is a worldwide leader in recyclable materials and processes, and continuously looks for ways to innovate. All challenges accepted!

PTI not only solves problems, but seeks out problems to solve

At the core, **PTI** is root-cause inspired and is dedicated to improving processes and the design of products that better lives. **PTI** takes the time to understand all components of the supply and distribution chains to deliver effective and profitable packaging design that is embraced by the end user.

PTI approaches engineering as an art and as a science

There's more to package design than aesthetics. In the packaging industry, **PTI** bridges the gap between elegant design and functionality. The **PTI** team evaluates each stage of the packaging process, from vetting a design to evaluating packaging products for peak performance and sustainability goals.

PTI has a passion for the pursuit of better packaging

There isn't an employee at **PTI** who picks up a package and doesn't inherently think about how to improve it. And, when the other companies can't deliver, **PTI** steps up to the challenge. **PTI** makes the impossible possible, by pursuing out-of-the box solutions.

PTI believes that micro decisions make macro impact

PTI's customers have realized that engaging **PTI** earlier in the package design process can significantly improve timelines and their bottom lines. **PTI's** detailed refinement process is proven to amend potential derailments before they jeopardize a project's success.

PTI Today

Today, **PTI** is recognized as a premiere PET technical development and support resource in the packaging industry.

Our 35 years of success has only been possible because of great people, starting with the key early team of Bob Deardurff, Scott Steele, Frank Semersky, and Betsy Brady, and the hundreds of owners, employees, and engineering co-op students who have followed and charted new paths since.

Together, we founded three successful sister companies that are still going strong, including **Phoenix Technologies International, PTI-Europe,** and **Preform Technologies**; we also founded or co-founded a number of joint venture companies with industry partners, including **INOVA Plastics, The Packaging Conference, Guardian Medical USA, Plastic Recovery Systems, Portare Leisure Products, PetWall LLC, Minus Nine Plastics,** and **PTI International**; we created 2 proprietary product businesses, **PTI Instruments** and **PT Healthcare Products**; we developed and/or licensed, sold, or used internally 17 proprietary products, including **Steel Coil Protective Rings, PortaBar™, Tru-Container™, StrataSys™ 3D Printer Material, OxyTraq™, TorqTraQ™, VisiTraQ™, LMS™, MuCell™, oPTI™ Foam Bottles, Virtual Prototyping™, PetWall Profiler™, Smart Blow Molding™, NFA™, PED2000™, SuperGreen™, LNOc™, LNOf™,** and **The Phoenix Process™**.

We are proud to have **PTI** employee names on more than 150 US and international patents, and we have served virtually every major PET machine and resin supplier, and every major US food and beverage brand owner, and we have done business in more than 25 countries around the world.

PTI employees have delivered more than 200 papers at major technical and business conferences and **PTI** has been instrumental in the startup and evolution of many of today's technical trade associations, including the **Association of Plastic Recyclers, Polymer Ohio,** the **Toledo Society of Plastic Engineers,** and the **Plastics Institute of America**.

PTI offers a complete array of technical services, including product design, prototyping, and testing, with a complete materials and product analytical testing laboratory, extensive lab-scale recycling capabilities and **PTI** offers manufacturing support services to all its customers. **PTI** also offers a completely virtual product design and simulation capability that has been employed across many industries and customers who come to **PTI** specifically to develop and innovate new products.

Through the years, **PTI** and the **PTI Family of Companies** have expanded numerous times from a one-person office at the corner of Canton and Speilbusch Avenues in Downtown Toledo in 1986, to its first rented office and laboratory facility at 333 14th Street in 1987, to our new 10,000 sq ft headquarters building at Wolf Creek Executive Park in 1994, followed quickly by our now 52,000 sq ft headquarters office/laboratory/storage facility in 1996, also in Wolf Creek, which is owned by **PTI** employees. Along the way, facilities were added in Bowling Green and Swanton OH and Yverdon Switzerland, adding a range of different capabilities.

PTI and **PTI** employees have also been important contributors to a great many community projects and organizations over our history. **PTI** remains an important supporter of the University of Toledo and the **UT College of Engineering**, where many **PTI** employees and Co-op students have trained over the years.

In June, 2019, Taiwan-based Far Eastern New Century Corp. (**FENC**) announced the acquisition of Phoenix Technologies International LLC, Bowling Green, Ohio. **Phoenix** is a **PTI** sister company founded in 1991 and is one of the leading recyclers of polyethylene terephthalate (PET) with the capability of processing more than 36,000 tons of rPET each year.

Phoenix is the third production site **FENC** has acquired in the U.S. over the last several years, including a PET production plant in West Virginia, a research and development center in Ohio and another PET plant in Texas.

In 2021 **PTI** and two other **PTI** sister companies, **PTI-Europe**, and **Preform Technologies**, also embarked on an exciting future, becoming collectively, the US and European Technical Partner with SIPA Industries, one of the leading and most innovative packaging equipment and service providers in the world and a long-time **PTI** ally. **SIPA** is headquartered in Italy and will now offer **PTI** sales and service opportunities around the world.

The PTI Family of Companies

Phoenix Technologies International (a PTI Company)

Website: https://phoenixtechnologies.net/

PTI "intrapreneurs" who conceived of, created, and ran Phoenix Technologies include Bob Deardurff, **PTI** VP and **Phoenix Technologies** CEO and Don Hayward, **PTI** Senior Technical Associate and First Plant Manager and General Manager of **Phoenix**.

Other former **O-I/PTI** personnel who also assumed major operational roles at **Phoenix Technologies** include Jack Ritchie, Henry Schworm, and Dennis Balduff.

Phoenix Technologies was established in 1992 and is now recognized as a global leader in recycled PET (rPET). The company manufactures clean, consistent, high-grade rPET resin pellets from post-consumer recycled plastic shipped from all over the world.

As the foremost manufacturer of rPET, **Phoenix** sets the benchmark for quality, technology, service and overall value. Phoenix' 90,000 square foot, state-of-the-art, Ohio recycling facility was designed from the ground up and produces 80 million pounds of rPET annually.

PET Bottles Containing up to 100% rPET

Using a fine-mesh filtration process or a fine-ground powder process, **Phoenix** is able to produce rPET which exceeds the industry's highest standards. Additionally, **Phoenix** prides itself on having ultra clean facilities, manufacturing quality products and having an impeccable safety record. More than a manufacturer, **Phoenix** thinks of itself as a partner to brand owners and to converters.

By leveraging **Phoenix's** strategic alliances with resin manufacturers, colorant and additive suppliers, processors, bottle producers and sheet extruders, Phoenix can give its customers a competitive advantage. With **Phoenix's** commitment to advanced technologies and unparalleled customer service, it is clear that customers' needs drive **Phoenix's** and **PTI's** packaging innovation.

PTI-Europe SARL (a PTI Company)

PTI-Europe was established in 1998 and initially operated as a separate but wholly owned **PTI** company in Lausanne, Switzerland for the purpose of conducting package and materials development projects for **PTI** customers located in Europe.

In 2003, **PTI-Europe** moved from Lausanne to picturesque Yverdon-les-Bains, Switzerland and expanded its Analytical Laboratory and added a joint venture permeability testing laboratory with MOCON Corporation. Shortly after the move, **PTI-Europe** added a Recycled PET Laboratory which was also available to the industry and the PET Technology Training Program became recognized as a standard industry training program for the European PET industry.

PTI "intrapreneurs" who conceived of, created, and managed **PTI – Europe SARL** include the late Frank Semersky, **PTI** VP Business Development, and Ann Roulin, the first General Manager of **PTI-Europe**.

When Thierry Fabozzi came from Nestle to assume the General Manager's role in 2012, he added the thin-wall molding and single serve capsule technologies to **PTI-Europe's** capabilities. Today Thierry is the President and CEO of **PTI** and the **PTI Companies.**

Frank Semersky, Helene Lanctuit, Jean-Claude Baumgartner, Christian Ducreux, Beatrice, Yen Andenmatten, Anne Roulin

Dana Giorgerini, Scott Steele, Stéphane Morier, Thierry Fabozzi, Antonio Farré, Pascal Sandoz, Nicolas Sframeli, Matthieu Larose, Jean-Claude Baumgartner, Christian Ducreux, Florence Baroni, Jean-Luc Roulin, Greg Fisher, Yen Andenmatten, Sylvie Magnin

Jean-Claude Baumgartner, Sylvie Vaucher, Vincent Le Guen, Yves-Eric Andenmatten, Helene Lanctuit, Christian Ducreux

The Packaging Conference (a PTI joint venture company)

Website: https://thepackagingconference.com

PTI "intrapreneurs" who conceived of, created, and ran the **Packaging Conference** include the late Frank Semersky, then **PTI** VP New Business Development and Ron Puvak, then **PTI** Marketing and Sales Director. **PTI's Packaging Conference** joint venture partner is SBA-CCA, founded by John Maddox, a former technical executive at Eastman Chemical, one of the industry's premier PET resin suppliers.

The **Packaging Conference** was created in 2008 as a joint venture between **PTI** and SBA-CCA as an annual industry conference that would update industry packaging professionals on the latest innovations in technology, design, and sustainability. Over the years, industry leaders from across the packaging supply chain, including consumer packaging suppliers, resin suppliers, technology providers, equipment manufacturers, and container, closure, and label manufacturers have gathered to facilitate connections and to share the latest consumer packaging innovations.

Networking Opportunities

The **Packaging Conference** exhibit area is always the focal point for investigating new technologies, businesses, and ideas. Each of the breakfasts, the morning and afternoon refreshment breaks, the Monday evening reception, and Tuesday luncheon are all designed for maximum networking.

In 2019, SBA-CCA became the sole owner of **The Packaging Conference**, although **PTI** still plays a major role in organizing and supporting what has become the number one annual packaging industry forum.

PTI Operations / Preform Technologies, Inc. (a PTI Company)

Preform Technologies website: http://www.preformtechnologies.com/

PTI "intrapreneurs" who conceived of, created, and managed **PTI Operations (Preform Technologies/PTLLC)** include Bob Deardurff, Dan Durham, and Jim Sheely.

Formed in late 2003, **PTLLC** is a manufacturing company that provides specialty and niche PET preforms and bottles to **PTI** and to **PTI** and **Phoenix** customers, as well as to the industry more broadly and, **Preform Technologies** can also offer specialty injection molding services for other packaging applications.

Preform Technologies is the extended production arm of **PTI**, supplying production and pre-production quantities of containers developed by **PTI**, and also supporting new product market launches and specialty product requirements, including specialty colors or materials.

Preform Technologies works hand in hand with **PTI** and **Phoenix Technologies** to offer design, development, production and recycle-content preforms and bottles which customers can't get anywhere else from a single source.

The fleet of **Preform Technologies** machines includes:

- Husky and SIPA injection machines
- Sidel SBO and SIPA stretch blow-molding machines
- Nissei Single Stage Injection/Blow molding machines
- Bekum extrusion blow molding machines

Guardian Medical USA

Web site: https://www.guardianmedicalusa.com

Guardian Medical is a joint venture between **Plastic Technologies, Inc.**, and **Spinal Balance**, founded by Dr. Anand Agarwal, a prominent internationally recognized orthopedic surgeon. **PTI** is a world-renowned plastics manufacturing and design firm that brings 35+ years in the food and beverage industry and **Guardian Medical** combines **PTI's** extensive plastics knowledge with medical device engineers to create modern and innovative sterile medical packaging solutions.

Guardian Medical designs, develops, manufactures, and sells proprietary sterile medical packaging and provides packaging services for medical implants, and the team of experienced engineering professionals at **PTI** and **Guardian** offer in-house injection molding and prototyping for seals, closures, and packaging validation.

Tracy Momany, a 30-year seasoned expert in plastic package development and the former Chief Technical Officer at **PTI** is CEO and Betsy Brady, a **PTI** founder is Chairman of the Board. Our joint venture partner, Dr. Anand Agarwal is the inventor of the technology and continues to work with Betsy and Tracy to secure additional future investment.

All in One Little Package

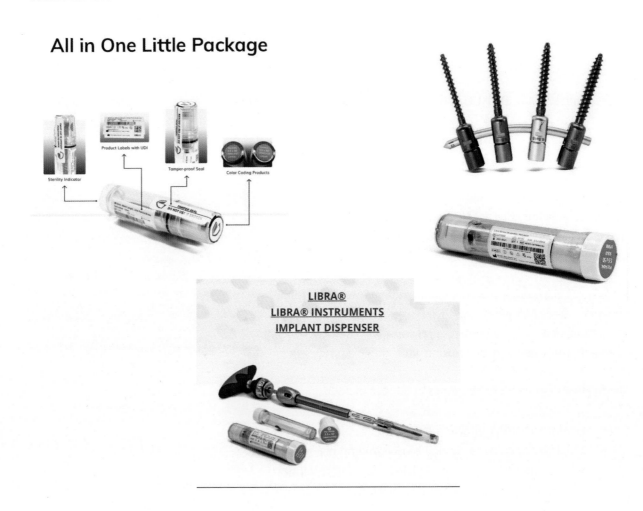

LIBRA®
LIBRA® INSTRUMENTS
IMPLANT DISPENSER

New (PET Technology) Business Development

As **PTI** continued to grow and to provide technical development services to virtually all companies involved in PET packaging, including brand owners, converters, resin suppliers, machinery manufacturers and raw material suppliers, **PTI** professionals developed several exciting and high potential technologies which were owned by **PTI,** and which offered potential sales or licensing opportunities.

To take advantage of these proprietary technologies, **PTI** created a **New Business Development** activity having the charter to pursue internal technology developments as business opportunities, either by joint venture, by licensing, or by creating independent, companies.

As a result, in 2001 **PTI** identified **Non-Contact International (NCI)** as a joint venture partner with the goal of developing a commercial prototype for an in-line bottle wall thickness measurement technology developed and patented by **PTI.**

The joint venture partners, **PTI and NCI**, formed a separate technology development and licensing company, **PETWall LLC,** which completed the development of the wall thickness gauge and licensed the technology to a global supplier of on-line inspection equipment, **Agr-TopWave.**

Today, **Agr-TopWave** manufactures, sells, and services online plastic bottle inspection equipment, trade-named **PETWall Vision™** which utilizes the original **PETWall™** wall thickness gauging systems technology.

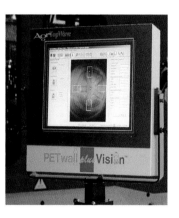

The early successful relationships between **PTI's** joint venture and license partners and **PTI** spurred additional instrumentation product developments by **PTI**, including a hand-held closure removal torque meter, **Torq-TraQ™**

PTI technical personnel also developed a novel oxygen permeation system, **OxyTraQ™**, which was licensed to **MOCON** for manufacture and sale as another instrument in the **MOCON** permeability instrumentation product line.

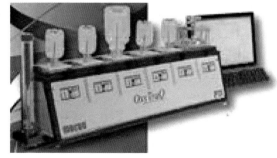

In 2003 **PTI** formed a joint venture with **Container Consulting Inc. (CCI)** for the purpose of commercializing and licensing another **PTI** proprietary technology, **Virtual Prototyping (VP)™,** to the industry. **VP™** is a computer simulation of PET preform/bottle design and processing, which allows the user to optimize the design of a preform and bottle combination prior to prototyping, by simulating the reheat-blow molding process using a computer-designed preform and then iterating the initial preform design by predicting the final bottle material distribution and performance.

This very powerful **VP™** software offers the industry higher speed and accuracy for routine bottle design and development and is now available for license from either **CCI** or from **PTI.**

As a further extension of this technology, **PTI** and **Agr-TopWave** together introduced **Smart Blow Molding™. SBM™** which combines **VP™** and **PETWall™** to provide closed loop feedback control to the blow molding process, by using continuous and real-time on-line wall thickness measurement as the metric for adjusting, optimizing, and controlling the blow molding machine's infrared heating system software, with the **VP™** software as the interface between the **PETWall™** gauge measuring system and the blow molding machine's IR heating system.

oPTI™ foamed PET technology was developed, patented, and commercialized in cooperation with Cincinnati Milacron (sells injection mold machines) and Faboha (sells injection molds). Coca-Cola successfully test-marketed the technology in Europe but it was never introduced in the US because of cost.

Other internally-developed technologies which were developed as license or joint venture opportunities, include the **NFA™,** a bottle imperfection detector which uses an ultrasonic method to "hear" defects as they are created during the blow molding process, a **Laser Measurement System (LMS)™,** which automatically creates a complete map of the outer dimensions of a bottle using laser detection of the outside surface in three-dimensional space, and a preform "free-blow" device for the laboratory, the **PED-2000™,** which allows the user to quickly and accurately determine "natural stretch ratio" for any bottle-making resin.

Monarch Analytical Laboratories
Founder – Dr. Dennis Brengartner
Former O-I R&D Manager

Website: https://www.westpharma.com/

In 1989 Dr. Dennis Brengartner, along with several others, left **O-I** to found **Monarch Analytical Laboratories Inc**. Initially **Monarch** remained located in the same laboratories that it had occupied in the (former) Owens-Illinois Technical Center on Westwood Avenue, and **Monarch** became a tenant of the University of Toledo since almost simultaneously with the formation of **Monarch**, Owens-Illinois donated that Technical Center facility to the University of Toledo.

Monarch's initial business focus was environmental smokestack testing, but **Monarch** also specialized in the physical testing of glass products and provided consulting and testing services related to the analytical chemistry of glasses. Because plastics were just becoming popular in the container industry, **Monarch** also provided analytical testing for the plastics packaging industry and, not surprisingly, **Monarch's** major initial customer was Owens-Illinois, an early leader in the plastics packaging industry. The only things that changed for **Monarch** employees were the name on the door and on the paycheck.

The original **Monarch** shareholders were Jim Hibbits, Charles Duck, Dr. Dennis Brengartner, Jim Hojnicki, Dr. Ernie Lippert, Dick Hansen, Ron Plenzler, Dick Beiswenger, Paul Sagert, Joe Grau, and Dr. Bill Greive, all former O-I employees.

After several years at that former O-I Tech Center facility, **Monarch** built its own laboratory building in Arrowhead Park in Maumee and moved to that facility in 1992.

The business grew rapidly and, over just several years, **Monarch** hired 30 employees, most with technical backgrounds. Over time, however, the focus of the business changed and by 1998, **Monarch** had completely exited the environmental testing business, which is what sustained Monarch in its early years.

By 1998, plastic packaging dominated the marketplace, particularly in the pharmaceutical industry but, because pharmaceutical products can react with the plastics in their packaging containers to both reduce the active product ingredients or to introduce plastic package additives into the pharmaceutical products, and because plastic packaging was being monitored by the FDA, **Monarch** was able to turn this plastic packaging "quality control problem" into a business opportunity, and **Monarch** became the "go to" testing laboratory for plastic packaging. Of course, **Monarch** continued to provide glass packaging materials analysis, but plastic packaging became the primary focus for **Monarch's** maturing business.

In 2005 **Monarch's** plastic testing and analysis business was acquired by **West Pharmaceutical Services**, one of Monarch's customers, but the glass testing services business continues under the name AGR in the former **Monarch** Arrowhead Park building.

At the time of its sale to **West Pharmaceutical Services** in 2005, annual revenues were $3.5M and **Monarch** employed 34 employees and the following article appeared on February 14, 2005, in the Lionville, PA Business Wire:

West Pharmaceutical Services, Inc. (NYSE: WST) announced its acquisition of **Monarch Analytical Laboratories, Inc.** of Maumee, Ohio in 2005. **Monarch** had 2004 sales of $3.0 million and **West** acquired all of the outstanding stock of **Monarch Analytical Laboratories** in exchange for cash, assumed liabilities and West shares totaling $5.6 million.

Monarch provides some of the largest U.S. pharmaceutical and medical device companies with a variety of analytical testing services from its facility, just outside of Toledo, Ohio and **West** provides analytical laboratory services from its facilities in Lionville, Pennsylvania. The combined laboratories operate under the name **WEST MONARCH Analytical Laboratories**. **West** continues to operate both the Pennsylvania and Ohio facilities. **WEST MONARCH Analytical Laboratories** offers a comprehensive menu of sophisticated analytical testing services for glass, plastics and elastomer packaging components to help global pharmaceutical manufacturers meet worldwide container/closure and packaging regulatory guidelines. **Monarch's** extensive capabilities and experience in glass and plastics testing complement **West's** extensive portfolio of services, most significantly, extractable and leachable testing for elastomer components, which **West** manufactures and represents its largest product group. Clients benefit from the combined resources and capabilities.

"**Monarch Analytical Laboratories** represented an excellent strategic fit that enabled **West** to provide its customers with a broader range of analytical testing services," said Herbert L. Hugill, President of the Americas Region, **West Pharmaceutical Services**. "**Monarch's** expertise and experience in testing nasal and inhalation devices brought added strengths to **West's** portfolio of services. Together, the two companies better assisted **West's** pharmaceutical clients to develop data that was critical to their product-related regulatory submissions."

West Pharmaceutical Services, Inc. is the world's premier manufacturer of standard-setting components and systems for injectable drug delivery. The company's products include stoppers and seals for vials, multi-piece tamper-resistant plastic closures and disposable components used in syringe, IV and blood collection systems. **West's** global customer base includes the world's leading manufacturers of pharmaceuticals, biologics and medical devices. Headquartered in Lionville, Pennsylvania, **West** employs 4,000 employees and supports its partners and customers from 50 locations throughout North America, South America, Europe, Mexico, Japan, Asia and Australia.

Electro-Plasma Inc. Global (EPI)
Co-Founder of EPI – Bernard W. (Bernie) Byrum
Former O-I Electrical Engineer

Bernie Byrum was born in Richmond, Indiana to parents Bernard W. Byrum Sr. and Violet May (Ryan) Byrum. He married his wife Joyce E. (Conarroe) Byrum on July 26, 1958, and they had two children, Karin and Glenn.

Bernie attended Richmond Senior High School where he played violin in the school orchestra. He served in the U.S. Army Reserves as a young man. Bernie attended Purdue University where he obtained both bachelor's and master's degrees in Electrical Engineering and later attended the University of Toledo, earning a master's in Business Administration. Bernie and his wife lived in Fort Wayne, Indiana for 11 years where he worked at ITT Industrial Co. as an Electrical Engineer. He moved with his family to Toledo in 1970 to work at Owens-Illinois as an Electrical Engineer.

Bernie left O-I in 1978 to found **EPI Global (Electro-Plasma Inc.)** in Millbury, Ohio. **EPI** was an **O-I Digi-Vue** spinoff and, after leaving **O-I**, **EPI** developed Plasma Displays for military and medical applications. Working with a major Korean company EPI developed the first 60-inch color plasma display in 1999. The company had over 20 patents relating to **Plasma Technologies** and **Non-Contact International (NCI)**, another **O-I** spin-off company, was in discussion to partner with **EPI** on an electro optics venture but that did not materialize.

Bernie was a member of the choir and the Joyful News Quartet at Church of Saint Andrew United Methodist in Toledo, OH and he was also a member of the Rotary Club of Toledo, through which he mentored high school students.

Non Contact International (NCI) and DLL Technologies LLC
Founders - Dennis Sturgill and Mike Charchol
Former O-I Senior Technical Associates

Website: http://www.noncontact.com/

Mike Charchol

Dennis Sturgill

Dennis Sturgill and Mike Charchol both worked in **O-I's Corporate Research Development Department** at the **O-I Technical Center** in Toledo for 25 years. In 1980, **O-I** formed **Automatic Inspection Devices (AID)** to commercialize machine vision technology developed for use in their production operations. At that time Machine Vision was a new technology incorporating CCD cameras and Micro Processors to provide non-contact inspection in manufacturing processes. Dennis was the Technical Director and Mike served as Operations Manager for **AID**.

Between 1980 and 1987 **AID** developed several unique products for gauging and defect inspection in the automotive, semi-conductor, packaging products, pharmaceutical and compact disk manufacturing industries.

In 1987 the KKR leveraged buyout of **O-I** resulted in the sale of **AID** to Medar Inc., a Farmington Hills, Michigan company which was forming a Machine Vision business.

Mike went to Medar and Dennis left **AID** to start a competing company.

Thus, Dennis Sturgill was the founding partner of **Non Contact International (NCI)** that officially opened in 1991 to develop electro-optical inspection systems for quality control in manufacturing. Over the next 7 years, **NCI** developed products for gauging steel tubing and defect inspection systems for ophthalmic lenses and CD optical media worldwide.

In 1998 Mike Charchol left Medar and joined **NCI**. Dennis and Mike acquired sole ownership of the **NCI** business in 2000 and the company focus changed from product commercialization to technology development.

The goal was to license intellectual property (IP) relating to automated non-contact inspection. Over the next 20 years **NCI** formed several partnerships resulting in the successful licensing of Automatic Inspection intellectual property.

One product developed was **PetWall**™ for gauging wall thickness of PET plastic containers. In 1999 **NCI** formed an LLC with **Plastic Technologies (PTI),** Holland Ohio, to jointly develop **PetWall**. A practical on-line PET container wall gauging solution had been elusive. **PetWall** was launched in 2001 and licensed to **AGR International**, Butler PA., for commercialization. As of 2020, **AGR** has produced and delivered more than 200 **PetWall** systems to manufacturing facilities worldwide.

NCI continued to provide gauging and inspection technology to the steel and ophthalmic lens industries through 2007. In 2003 they started a new development to gauge the thickness of transparent curved and flat products in the glass and plastic market.

In 2002 a patent was issued for a new technology **DLLS.**, using diffuse line light in camera systems to make exact optical corrections for prism and parallax effects that normally cause errors in other methods used for thickness measurement. In 2006 **NCI** formed **DLL Technologies (DLL)** and Dr. Clifton George Daley, who also had worked at the **O-I Technical Center** with Mike and Dennis and had collaborated with them in developing **DLLS**, also became a partner in **DLL Technologies**.

Unlike **PetWall** which was designed to gauge a specific product, **DLLS** had applicability in many different product markets. Over the next few years, **DLLS** technology was introduced for gauging wall thickness in glass tubing, ampoules, vials, plastic preforms and medical tubing. Products developed included **WallEye**™, **CentriScan**™ and **THIKCHEK**™.

In 2012, **DLL** entered into an agreement to supply **THIKCHEK** technology to **AVID Vision**, a Portsmouth, NH. machine vision company. Over 80 **THIKCHEK** systems are in use worldwide today and a second generation is under development by **DLL** and **AVID**.

In 2020 **DLL** entered into a contract with **AVID** that will eventually transfer all **DLL** IP to **AVID**.

Anatrace
Founders - Drs. Don Gray, Mel Keyes, and Barry Watson
Former O-I R&D Managers and Senior Associates

Website: https://www.anatrace.com/

Don Gray, Mel Keyes, and Barry Watson founded **Anatrace Inc.** in 1985, after accepting employee buyout proposals from Owens-Illinois. At the time of its founding, the company developed sensors for blood acidity and blood electrolytes used in diagnostic laboratory equipment. The men worked on the technology while at Owens-Illinois and bought the rights to it when they left.

Over the years, Dr. Gray helped lead the company into manufacturing. He held more than 30 patents and was recognized as a 50-year member of the American Chemical Society.

After receiving a doctorate in organic chemistry from the University of Colorado, he worked for the Denver Research Institute and Martin Marietta, before moving to Toledo and joining O-I.

Research facilities, academic institutions, and industrial customers worldwide counted on **Anatrace** for high-purity detergents and lipids, and **Anatrace** was also regarded as a high-quality producer of membrane protein used in structural biology. **Anatrace** products were known for their uniquely pure molecules and the exacting chemistry behind them, and the company was recognized for developing compounds designed to disrupt cell membranes and to create and produce products that stabilized or solubilized unstable macromolecules and proteins. **Anatrace** was also known for conducting structural studies, carrying out functional biology work, and for handling chemical synthesis projects that always yielded incredibly reliable results, which is why scientific publications consistently cited **Anatrace** an average of over 400 times per year.

Along with an extensive portfolio of products, **Anatrace** chemists developed specialized solutions tailored to meet customers' unique specifications and **Anatrace** also provided custom synthesis services and expert analytical work to aid customers' own research and development teams

In 2013 **Anatrace** was acquired by StoneCalibre, a private equity investment company, and was combined with several other small life science companies to create Calibre Scientific, which today is a portfolio of niche life science companies, across various key verticals, that have an unrivaled ability to address the unique challenges of their respective markets. Through a combination of acquisitions and organic growth, Calibre Scientific's global reach extends into over 100 countries, empowering customers all over the world. Headquartered in Los Angeles, California, Calibre Scientific continues to grow across a wide array of verticals and geographies, further diversifying its product offering and global footprint to laboratories around the world.

AIM Packaging
Founder – Frank Harris
Former O-I Plastic Products Division Sales Manager

Frank was born in Lincolnton, NC on January 15, 1933, the son of Walter Lee and Pinkey Marbel (Meetze) Harris. He grew up in Lincolnton, NC and attended the University of North Carolina at Chapel Hill graduating in 1955 with a BS in Industrial Relations. He was a member of Phi Kappa Sigma, and a cheerleader.

On September 29, 1956, he married Virginia "Susie" Welles Draper in Maumee, OH.

He began his career in sales and sales management for **Owens-Illinois Glass Co**. In 1969, he co-founded **Aim Packaging Inc.,** a major producer of, and plastic bottle supplier to, Proctor and Gamble, Helene Curtis, Clairol, Bristol Myers, Drackett and others, with five plants nationwide. In 1984, he became president of the **Plastic Bottle Institute**, a division of the **Society of Plastics Industry**. As his career in plastics was winding down, in 1985 he founded and became president of **Green Cove Development Corp**. which today is being operated by his children. The corporation built and sold 400 condominiums, operated **Wild Wings Marina** and **RV Park** as well as other related small businesses. He was a member of both the **Young Presidents Organization** and then **Chief Executive Organization**. In 1986, he was elected to the board of the **Institute of Private Enterprise**, part of the business school at Chapel Hill.

He served on many boards including Blue Cross of Ohio, Toledo Humane Society, Brazeway Inc. of Adrian, MI, **Plastic Technologies** of Holland, OH, Continental Glass and Plastics of Chicago, American Seniors Golf Association, International Seniors Amateur Golf Society where he was vice-president, Three Score and Ten Golf Society, the 200 Club of Gentlemen Golfers, The Forum Club of Naples, FL, and the Boys and Girls Club of Collier County, FL.

Frank was an avid sportsman. He played tennis and platform tennis, fished and hunted birds across the USA, Spain, Scotland, Ireland, Canada, Argentina and Mexico. He belonged to Erie Marsh, and Sand Beach Shooting Clubs, Ottawa Skeet Club, and Rockwell Trout Club. His passion was golf which he played with a low handicap for over 50 years. He won 20 club championships, had 8 holes in one, once owned **Spuyten Duyval Golf Course** in the Toledo Ohio area, served as a panelist for Golf Digest and Golf Magazine to rank the top 100 courses in the world for over 10 years, was a panelist for the World Club Championship and was named one of the top joke tellers in golf, by Golf Digest.

He was a member of Pine Valley Golf Club, Royal Poinciana Golf Club of Naples, Hole-in-the-Wall Golf Club of Naples and Birchwood Farms Golf and Country Club of Harbor Springs, MI.

First Solar and Willard and Kelsey
Co-Founder – James Heider
Former O-I Technical Manager

Jim was born on January 28, 1936, to Elmer and Kathryn (Chisholm) Heider at their home at Willard and Kelsey Streets in East Toledo. Jim was the second oldest of six siblings. His parents raised him to be a man of character, with a strong work ethic and a love for family. With a mechanic for a father, Jim learned much about tinkering with cars and how to fix things.

Growing up, Jim loved sports and became a standout athlete in football, basketball and track for his alma mater, Waite High School. Jim was named First Team All-City in football and All-State linebacker. He set scoring records in basketball and for the shotput and discus. For his athletic prowess, Jim was inducted into the Waite Athletic Hall of Fame as part of the first class in 1972 and into the Toledo City League Hall of Fame in 1992.

He was a National Honor Society member, earning an academic scholarship to study at the University of Toledo where he obtained his bachelor's degree in mechanical engineering. He was hired by **Owens-Illinois** and was first to be offered a fellowship to study plastics engineering at Princeton University. Jim excelled in his studies, completing his master's degree in nine months.

At **O-I**, Jim helped to pioneer the development of plastic bottles for beverages and detergents earning numerous patents. He retired from **O-I** as technical director after 27 years.

After **O-I,** Jim worked at **Glasstech, Inc.** as VP of Development and Engineering. He helped develop innovative processes for manufacturing glass for automobiles and buildings and operated his own plastics consulting business. Later, he became one of the principles in both **Solar Cells** and the **Willard & Kelsey Solar Group**. In all, he earned over 150 patents worldwide and in 1995, he was inducted as a Distinguished Waite Alumnus.

Coexcell
Founder - Bob Huebner
Former Manager of O-I Plastic Drum Operations

 Robert "Bob" Huebner, president of **U.S. Coexcell, Inc.,** in Maumee, Ohio, stood 6 feet, 7 inches tall, towering above everyone else not only physically but possessing the fortitude and charisma of a natural born leader. He was a devoted husband, father, grandfather, son, and brother; an astute businessman; and an exceptional athlete. Whatever the endeavor, if Bob decided that he was committed, he was all in with a passion and determination to succeed few could match. Born on November 3, 1954, Bob grew up in West Toledo, attended Monac Elementary School and graduated from Whitmer High School ('72), where he starred on the basketball team. His senior year, he was named first team in the former Great Lakes League, a feat he cherished. Bob earned a scholarship to Wittenberg University in Springfield, Ohio, where he continued his success in basketball and completed a degree in accounting. Following graduation, in 1976, Bob returned to Toledo and joined the auditing department at **Owens-Illinois, Inc.** In 1978, he was asked to direct the company's Plastic Drum Division, where he remained for 15 years. During this time, he earned an MBA from the University of Toledo.

In 1993, Bob and Harley Cramer, a co-worker from **O-I**, founded their own plastic drum business in Arrowhead Park, which they named **U.S. Coexcell**. Bob's energy level was such that while **U.S. Coexcell** was growing, he became president of **VITEC**, a Detroit automotive fuel systems supplier. He remained at **VITEC** for 10 years, commuting to Detroit, while continuing to manage **U.S. Coexcell**. Beginning in 2005, Bob directed his business efforts entirely toward **U.S. Coexcell**. With his aggressive approach to sales and marketing and an ability to secure niche markets, the company prospered.

Mr. Huebner was also vice president of the **Chemical Allied Industries** of Northwest Ohio and in 2007 he was inducted into the Entrepreneurial & Business Excellence Hall of Fame.

Bob remained active in sports throughout his life. In his 20s, he played federation basketball with some of the city's best players. He was an ardent supporter of the UT basketball team, and he loved the Detroit Tigers. Bob was an excellent golfer and long-standing member of Toledo Country Club. He had three holes-in-one, including two in 2010. But the one he treasured most happened in April 2008, on No. 17 at Toledo Country Club with his son, Jake, playing alongside. A note to his son inscribed on the trophy holding the ball reads: "My best playing partner in the world." First and foremost, Bob was a family man.

He was married on January 28, 1989, to Renee (Morrin). He coached his children's sports teams. He loved to host family dinners, especially when he manned the grill, a favorite hobby. Bob enjoyed boating with family and friends, cruising up the Maumee River, and fishing in Lake Erie. Bob was often teased for his meticulous nature, yet it was his quest for perfection that helped him succeed in everything he did.

Polymer Institute at the University of Toledo
Founder – Dr. Saleh Jabarin
Former O-I Plastics R&D Manager

In 1979, Clarence D. (Doc) Pawlicki, a Navy veteran and a 1950 chemical engineering graduate of the University of Toledo who held increasingly important management and production jobs in the International and Lily-Tulip Divisions of **O-I** was designated as what turned out to be the last Technical Director and Vice President of Corporate Research at **Owens Illinois (O-I)**.

In 1985, as **O-I** was eliminating its corporate research technical activities, Doc Pawlicki was named by then Ohio Governor Celeste as the Director of the Ohio Department of Development, which turned out to be fortuitous for both the University of Toledo and for my friend and colleague, Dr. Saleh Jabarin, who at the time was managing **O-I's** plastic materials research activities, under the direction of Doc Pawlicki.

After completing the dissolution of the Plastics Materials Research activity at **O-I** and as he was assuming the Directorship of the Ohio Department of Development, Doc Pawlicki seized upon an opportunity and proposed to **Owens-Illinois** and to the University of Toledo (UT), the establishment of a **Polymer Research Center** at the University.

After some negotiations, an agreement was signed between **O-I** and UT, whereby **O-I** would transfer its plastics materials laboratory equipment to UT and whereby UT would create a location for a new **Polymer Institute** and Dr. Saleh Jabarin would transfer from **O-I** to UT and become the Director of that new **Polymer Institute.**

The University, at the time, was represented by Dr. Harold Allen, Vice President for Research at UT, and **O-I** was represented by Dr. David Moore, then Vice President of Research in the **Plastic Products Division** at **O-I**.

When the agreement was signed, the establishment of the **Polymer Institute** was announced on the front page of the Toledo Blade on January 1, 1987.

The name of the institute was decided on after consultation with then UT College of Engineering Dean, Dr. Les Lahti.

According to the agreement, **O-I** agreed to continue to pay Dr. Jabarin's salary for two years, and UT agreed to make Dr. Jabarin a fulltime faculty member of the College of Engineering after 18 months.

During the month of January 1987, Dr. Jabarin recommended to Dean Lahti that UT should transfer the entire trained **O-I Polymer Research** staff to UT, including Mrs. Elizabeth Lofgren, Dr. Wendel Kollen, Mr. Sharad Shah, Mr. Michael Mumford, Dr. Michael Cameron, and Dr. Long Fei Chang. Mrs. Denise Busdecker also transferred and was hired as the administrative assistant for the institute.

The new **UT Polymer Institute** initially operated from the Levis Commons campus of **Owens Illinois** in Perrysburg for six months, and then moved to a newly renovated facility on the campus of the University of Toledo, which happened to also be a former O-I research facility located right across the street from the **O-I Technical Center** and on the UT campus.

The new **UT Polymer Institute** was intended to serve as a center for research and development in polymers and plastics technology, as well as an education and industrial training center for polymer science and engineering. Seven years later, the **PET/Polyester Industrial Consortium** was founded with the aim of discovering new applications and processing and property improvements for polyester materials.

Since 1994, membership in the **PET/Polyester Industrial Consortium** has included 23 national and international corporations and research has been conducted on interrelationships among material properties, fabrication processes, and end-use performance. In addition to the work done within the Consortium, topics such as properties, structure, processing and product applications have been explored by more than 70 MS and PhD students who have since graduated and found great success in the plastics and chemical fields. Since 2014, and after Dr. Jabarin retired, the **Polymer Institute** has been directed by Dr. Joseph Lawrence.

While at UT, Dr. Jabarin served as the Director of the **Polymer Institute** and was also a tenured Professor of Chemical and Environmental Engineering at UT. He holds a bachelor's degree in Chemistry from Dartmouth College, a master's degree in Polymer Science from Brooklyn Polytechnic Institute and a Ph.D. in Polymer Science and Engineering from the University of Massachusetts. He had 15 years of industrial plastic research and development experience before joining UT, ranging from fundamental plastics R&D and product development to manufacturing start-up and support. Prior to joining the University of Toledo in 1987, Dr. Jabarin was manager of the **Plastics Technology Department** at **Owens-Illinois**. There he served as a principal researcher and authored a number of patents and trade secrets which resulted in successful commercial products and licensed technologies at **Owens-Illinois**.

Dr. Jabarin was the driving force in planning, organizing, and financing the 1987 establishment of the **Polymer Institute**. He initiated and coordinated both the industrial and university contributions and responsibilities. As the Institute's Director, he was responsible for planning, budgeting, staffing, directing, supervising and allocation of the Institute's technical resources and for directing and conducting research and development projects for the industry on a contractual basis.

Dr. Jabarin was recognized with the title of "Distinguished University Professor" at the University of Toledo in 2008.

In 2021, Saleh completed and published his very interesting life story titled "The Journey – Finding Relevance Through the Pursuit of Learning." You can purchase Saleh's book at BookBaby.com (https://store.bookbaby.com/book/the-journey5)

B&B Box
Founders - Bill Laimbeer Sr. and Bill Laimbeer Jr.
Former VP O-I Forest Products Division and his son

William Laimbeer Sr. grew up in southern England. In 1956, he married Joan Waldon and moved to Oahu when Bill was stationed at the Marine Corps base in Kaneohe. Bill and Joan left Hawaii in 1957 and moved to Cambridge where Bill attended Harvard and their first child was born.

In 1959 Bill was hired by **Owens-Illinois, Inc.** as a **Forest Products Division** sales representative in Jacksonville, Florida. Thus, began a long and distinguished career in the paper industry. In 1962, he was appointed sales manager of the Orlando office and two years later he was Manager of Product and Market Development for the division. From 1966 to 1971 he was assigned to the Chicago box plant where he served as sales manager before becoming general manager. He was promoted to general manager of the Los Angeles box plant in January 1971 and eventually the whole Pacific coast region. After returning to Toledo, OH in 1975, Bill was appointed a vice president of the division and general manager of all box operations. He was elected a VP in 1976 and named GM of the **Forest Products Division** in 1981. He was elected to the board of directors in 1984. He finished his career in the paper industry with executive positions at **Great Northern Nekoosa Corp.**, **Georgia Pacific**, and **Stone Container** after the sale of **Owens-Illinois' Forest Products division** in 1987.

In retirement, Bill was actively involved in numerous charities that focused on education, establishing scholarship funds and building schools. He served on several charitable boards including Junior Achievement, RCMA, the Community Foundation, the Ronald McDonald Care Mobile and The Clery Foundation. He was a member of St. Mark's Episcopal Church and participated in many of their charitable endeavors.

He was recognized for his charitable work in 2010 when he was named a Southwest Florida Philanthropist of the Year.

In addition to his charity work, Bill will be remembered as a proud, devoted and vocal Democrat. Often the only Democrat amongst his friends and golfing buddies, Bill took great delight in stirring the pot, poking the bear and whatever it took to confuse and confound the enemy. He gave generously to female democratic candidates around the country and hoped to elect a woman president one day.

In 1993, the younger Bill Laimbeer (Detroit Pistons and Notre Dame basketball player) founded **Laimbeer Packaging Corp.**, known as the **B&B Box Company**, and which he owned with his father and other investors. The company made boxes in a factory in Detroit, and later added a second factory in Melvindale, Michigan, that made corrugated boxes. Bill Laimbeer Jr. ran the company, which had 240 employees and $60 million in projected sales in 1995. The Laimbeers sold the Detroit plant in 2000 and focused the company on the large box and heavy weight container manufacturing business. The Laimbeers left the business entirely in October of 2001.

Brockway Moran Partners
CEO – Randall Litten
Former O-I VP and General Manager

 Randall graduated from Ohio University with a BS and from the University of Toledo with an MBA.

He joined the **Owens-Illinois Glass Container Division** in 1965 as Sales Development Manager and rose through various sales roles to Product Manager before being named Director of Sales and Marketing for the R&D start-up **Polyester Beverage Bottle Operation (PBO)** in 1974.

He was promoted to General Manager of this operation in 1977 when it was a three-machine R&D operation and served as GM until he was promoted to **Closure Division** General Manager in 1980, at which time **PBO** had grown to a 5-plant $140 million commercial business which had generated $20 million in profits over the prior 3 years.

From the **Closure Division** general management position, Randall was subsequently promoted to general manager of the **Plastic Products Division** and to **O-I's** largest division, the $ 1 billion **Glass Container Division.**

In 1987, Randall left **O-I** to become President of **Atlantis Plastics, Inc**, a $54 million mini-conglomerate that was in the process of going public. When he left six years later to become CEO of **Atlantis Films**, a stretch film unit of **API**, the company had grown to $200 million.

In 1995, Randall became Operations Executive of **Trivest Inc**, a private equity firm, a role in which he provided acquisition expertise and portfolio oversight to several companies.

In 1998, along with colleagues from **Trivest**, Randall founded a new private equity firm, known as **Brockway Moran and Partners**. This firm became one of the premier private equity firms in the Southeast, raising funds totaling $1.3 billion, ranking in the top quartile of funds of its vintage.

Randall has now been involved in private equity investing for over thirty years. During this time, he has successfully partnered with numerous management teams to expand industrial, consumer and service companies into larger and more diverse enterprises, and he has served as director on many boards, including Norwesco, Inc., Cosmetic Essence, Inc. Woodstream Corporation, MW Industries, Inc, Celeste Industries and Penda Corporation. Randall is now retired but remains an Advisory Partner for **Brockway Moran**.

Randall and his wife of 60 years, Georgette, live in Miami where he has a leading role in serving the homeless community in downtown Miami. He has also been active in the leadership of his church and has served on the Board of the YMCA. His hobbies include boating and active involvement in continuing education classes at the University of Miami.

Light Works LLC
Founder of Light Works LLC – Spencer Luster
Former O-I Senior Optical Engineer

Spencer Luster, a physicist, started **Light Works** after leaving **OI (AID)** in the 90's. **Light Works** has worked with **Non Contact International (NCI)** on several projects and **Light Works** develops and produces Telecentric lenses, Optical splitters and Hypercentric/Pericentric lenses. **Light Works** is also a supplier to Edmund Optics, a global manufacturer of optical technology.

Spencer has been recognized as an expert in machine vision optics and lighting design since 1985. He is the former Chairman of the Board of Advisors to SME's Machine Vision Association, holds seven patents for optical systems, and continues to develop new optical products for the machine vision industry.

Light Works specialties include:

- Hypercentric/Pericentric Lens Design and Supply
- Telecentric imaging and lighting systems design
- Optical view splitter design and production
- General contrast enhancement techniques
- Polarization synthesis and analysis
- IR and near IR imaging and thermography
- Spectral analysis and synthesis
- Sensor design and modification for special purposes
- Mechanical design and analysis
- Physical measurements and gauging

HiTech Polymers
CEO – Dr. Gerald W. Miller
Former O-I Plastics R&D Manager

Education:
M.S. Organic Chemistry, 1957, Duquesne University
PH.D. Physical Chemistry, 1959, Duquesne University
M.A. Religion, 1990, Mt. St. Mary's Seminar

Gerald Miller Patents: https://patents.justia.com/inventor/gerald-w-miller

After twenty years of working in various segments of the polymer business with Mobay Chemical, the DuPont Co., **Owens Illinois**, and with the encouragement of my wife, Tommie, I started **HiTech Polymers** in 1981. The objective of our business was to provide polymer solutions for custom needs that were not being satisfied by existing sources. At that time, it was difficult to find, collaborate, and source specific types of polymers. We began our adventure using twin screw extruders from Werner Pfleiderer with both underwater pelletizers as well as conventional strand pelletizers.

We initially developed technology for combining immiscible polymers and additives for specific functions which necessitated using different extruder and die designs with new available equipment. These types of equipment gave us a head start in making highly filled compositions for several applications, including glass filled thermoplastics, such as PP, PET, PUR, PS and PE, at loadings of up to 50%. Color concentrates in specific resins were readily made to compete with larger compounders.

Our customers wanted specific sizes and shapes for their use, resulting in our initiating development of micropellets from most thermoplastic resins for several companies. Micropellets were used for making molded foam parts, mainly for automotive bumpers, which was a significant business opportunity.

Water soluble polymers were not easy to produce on our equipment, but we were able to make product from polyvinyl alcohol, vinyl alcohol copolymers and starch which were then converted into sheet products. Eventually, we turned our attention to reactive polymer processing for polymers which made reactions of polymer functionality a new area of endeavor. Our extruders became reactors for specific compounds, and we began designing and building our own auxiliary equipment to increase our ability to grow as a specialty supplier and increase our production rates.

Recycled polymers provided small programs for understanding their use after a five-year contract for recycling clear PVC. Other thermoplastics were also converted for use in polymer concentrates.

We spent a lot of time recruiting technical people who could think and create on the edge of all the polymer work being done in larger companies. We were fortunate to find a few of these types of people as well as consultants whom I had known from earlier employment. They helped us to teach our new hires to "think out of the box" and do the unusual.

From 1983 to 1994, we moved to larger plant space twice prior to building our 55,000 sq ft facility in Hebron, KY, in which we enlarged our production with more equipment and people. We worked with larger companies to make additional materials and became a part of the production team at some customers' plants. This collaborative work was done with mutual respect and confidentiality agreements.

During the next ten years our growth was accomplished with new products, new services, new people and tolling opportunities. As a specialty business, we were approached by several companies to integrate our business with their needs. We were able to see a mutual advantage to working with the 3M company, and agreed to become part of their Fluoropolymer Division in 2008.

I wish to thank all those with whom I have had the pleasure and enjoyment of being a part of their creativity and work. In particular, may I thank my wife, Tommie, my daughter, Michelle, a polymer engineer, Mr. Harald Lutzmann, a long-time personal friend and consultant, and Dr. Donald Uhlmann, professor of Material Science MIT. They were a wonderful group, and may God bless them all.

Contributed by Dr. Gerald Miller

Northwood Industries
Founder of Northwood Industries – James Miller
Former O-I Electrical Engineer

Jim and Kurt Miller

Jim Miller left **O-I** and started **Northwood Industries**, a specialty machining operation, in 1968. Today, **Northwood Industries** operates in Perrysburg and provides precision machining and fabrication. Jim officially retired in 2002 and **Northwood** is now run by his son Kurt who has been a partner from the beginning.

Northwood Industries is a multi-generation family business established in 1968 in Northwood Ohio. **Northwood's** founder, Jim Miller, started the machining business in his garage working evenings and weekends, after he left **O-I**. His first equipment purchases were a used lathe, a milling machine, a saw and a welder.

Kurt Miller

However, Jim leveraged his natural mechanical skills and focused on making prototype parts for development engineers, turning their designs into components for testing and manufacturing. He also provided maintenance machining services to local companies.

Although Jim retired in 2002, the company continues to be family owned and operated. Today, **Northwood** provides precision machined component parts, mechanical assemblies and engineering design services to manufacturing companies throughout the North America, Europe and Asia and they have maintained a number of customer relationships dating back to 1970, including the Hirzel Canning Company in Northwood as well as Helm Instrument Company in Maumee.

Northwood's business grew by serving its customers and by blending the talent of its highly trained machinists with state-of-the-art computer aided design and machining technologies. **Northwood** today serves many industries, including the solar energy, automotive, plastics, food and medical industries and 65% of Northwood's sales come from outside the state of Ohio. During **Northwood's** 47-year history, the company has relocated several times to gain more space to allow it to meet its customer's needs. In 1988, **Northwood** moved from Jim's garage in Northwood to a small industrial building in North Toledo and in 1999, to accommodate its growing business, Jim and Kurt returned to Wood County and built a modern machining facility on 2-acre parcel in the Cedar Business Center in Perrysburg Township. In 2013, **Northwood** completed a 12,000 square foot expansion and currently operates in a 23,500 square foot facility and employs 24 full-time skilled tradesmen and support personnel.

Nugent Orchards
Co-Owner - Duane Nugent
Former O-I Senior Chemical Engineering Associate

Duane Nugent joined **Nugent Orchards** as a full-time partner in 1989 after retiring from **O-I** and after completing the plastic wire insultation research, development, and commercialization project at **Plastic Technologies, Inc.** and after helping to start up the **Plastic Recovery Systems (PRS)** commercial operation

Duane's grandfather, Herbert Nugent, had purchased the northwest 40 acres of **Nugent Orchards** in December 1918. At that time the property had only a few acres of apples. Before working the farm, Herbert decided to try his hand at factory work in Sheboygan, Wisconsin. He met his wife Emira Olson while living in Wisconsin. They were married, started their family and decided to move back to Michigan, and lived in a small home on his farm they once called the bachelor pad.

Herbert later purchased the adjacent 60-acre house and farm to the east of his property. Grandpa and grandma, and their three children, Betty, Imogene, and Harry worked the farm together. As a young man, Harry purchased the farm from his parents. Along with cherries and apples, Harry raised potatoes, cauliflower, and pickles. He also leased muck ground near Beulah and raised vegetables for a while.

Harry married Kathryn Joy in August 1960. In the span of five years, he and Kathryn had five children, John, Brian, Scott, and twins, Pete & Carol. Together Harry and Kit raised kids and fruit! Everyone was always welcomed into their home with coffee and homemade desserts. They expanded the cherry and apple production taking advantage of auto workers families on summer vacation to pick cherries – what was work to the family, was fun for vacationers! This type of thinking led Harry to more innovative ways of farm production. Planting apple trees close together, building greenhouses for early sweet cherries, and always willing to share his knowledge with others has left an impression. Upon Kit and Harry's passing, they left a great farm, a lot of fond memories of farm life, and a legacy to live up to.

The children decided to keep farming and like their dad, they looked for other ways to utilize the family farm. A fall pumpkin patch and farm market, where people could take a wagon ride, get a pumpkin, and pick some apples were added. One of their nephews and his wife got married on the farm. The following week they held their dad's memorial service, which showed them a whole new opportunity of offering a venue for weddings or special events. Starting in 2019, they offered the farm as a location for those special events where the public could use the farm for their special day and get a glimpse of the farm life.

Nugent Orchards will continue its tradition of commercial apple and cherry production along with providing opportunities for the public to enjoy the farm, pick their own fruit, and have fun on the farm while doing it.

SEM-COM Company, Inc.
Founder of SEM-COM – Larry Pfaender
Former O-I Electrical Engineer

Larry Pfaender

Lawrence (Larry) V. Pfaender was raised in Ottawa Hills, and after college and military service, married Donna Marie Coy, his Pi Beta Phi sweetheart from the University of Toledo, in 1950.

Larry graduated from the University of Toledo (Alpha Sigma Phi) with a B.S. in Mechanical Engineering, and then joined **Owens-Illinois**, where he worked for more than 31 years.

In 1984, he left **O-I** to found **SEM-COM** and served as Chairman and CEO of **Sem-Com Company, Inc.**, which produced specialty glass, sealing glass, and glass powders and operated in Toledo for more than 30 years. Today, however, **SEM-COM's** products are made and sold by a company in Texas. Larry's son, Mike, worked with him as a partner.

Larry's entire technical career focused on integrating glass and ceramic technology with rapidly advancing digital and electronic technology, a field in which he made major contributions. His innovative work resulted in 21 patents in his name, which included important advances in fiber optic and flat panel display technology.

Larry was intensely patriotic, and his devotion to his country included serving in the U.S. Navy in WWII aboard the USS Severn, which participated in the battles of Leyte Gulf and Okinawa.

Southeastern Container and The Coca-Cola Company
Founder – Richard Roswech
Former O-I Plastics Plant Manager

Website: http://www.secontainer.com/

 **O-I** Employees who moved to Coca-Cola to help found and run **Southeastern Container** and several other Coca-Cola Coop PET bottle manufacturing facilities include Dick Roswech, John Johnson, Henry Pinto, John Bombace, Doug Wehrkamp, Tom Francis, and Bruce Sampson

Founded in 1982, **Southeastern Container (SEC)** is organized as a Coca-Cola PET bottle manufacturing co-op. The company was originally organized by a group of Coca-Cola bottlers in the Southeastern United States to meet their need for cost effective PET soft drink bottles and **SEC** produces and sells containers, at cost, for the exclusive use of Coca-Cola bottlers, who are the owners and/or participating members of the cooperative. **Southeastern Container** is proud of its company history and makes every effort to provide good working conditions and a pleasant work environment. The individual success of each employee is important to the success of the overall business, and all of the **SEC** employees working together as a unified team build the foundation of a successful relationship and create an environment that helps the Company achieve its mission to "Provide environmentally sustainable packaging solutions that exceed the expectations of the Coca-Cola Bottling community and other valued customers."

Prior to **SEC**, PET bottles were purchased from merchant suppliers at a much higher cost. The availability of products from the co-op substantially reduced the cost of a key raw material to the member bottlers, in addition to creating a company that has become a technology leader in the PET beverage industry.

The Company's first plant, including injection molding and blow-molding, was opened in 1982 in Enka, North Carolina, near Asheville. Over the years, the Company has experienced substantial growth, largely due to the addition of member bottlers throughout the Eastern and Midwestern US. The Winchester, VA plant was opened for injection molding and blow-molding in 1992, and Bowling Green, OH was added with injection molding and blow-molding in 1999. In 2000 the Company started the Cleveland, TN operation as a blow-molding plant, and in 2005 the Company relocated blow-molding out of the Enka, NC facility and opened the Kings Mountain, NC plant, creating additional blow-molding capacity in Kings Mountain and increasing space for the expansion of injection molding in Enka.

The operation of efficient injection molding and blow molding equipment is key to the success of SEC and close working relationships are maintained with the Company's primary manufacturers of injection and blow molding equipment worldwide. In addition, SEC is committed to supporting container recycling and recovering through the use of post-consumer recycled content in their products and SEC looks to the future while continuing to provide products, services, and packaging solutions to the Coca-Cola bottling community, utilizing the core values of *Commitment, Sustainability, Teamwork, Accountability, and Trust.*

Fremont Plastics
Founder - Paul Rothschild
Former O-I VP, Plastic Products Division Technical Director
and VP O-I International Operations

After leaving **Owens-Illinois** in 1984, Paul Rothschild planned to enter the large part blow molding business, based on the industry trends at that time. During the ensuing months of planning and visiting machine makers, he became aware that a molder in Fremont, OH was for sale.

An acquisition team was formed consisting of Paul, his wife, Rona, Claude Young, owner of an injection molding company, and Don Smith, formerly of the Plastic Drum Operations at **Owens-Illinois** and who was at that time employed by a plastic drum manufacturing operation in the Chicago area.

After a visit to **Fremont Plastics** and after discussion with the owners and current customers, the team decided to proceed with the acquisition, rather than to embark on a green field startup.

Fremont Plastics, Inc. Management Team, Don Smith, Rona Rothschild, Paul Rothschild, Joe Debortoli, and Don Staczek

The existing **Fremont Plastics** operation had sales of about $3 million with 35 employees and its primary customers were Little Tikes, a toy manufacturer, and the Ford Motor Company. Although **Fremont,** at the time, was disqualified from new business at Ford based on quality issues, discussions with Ford offered a reasonable time frame to correct those problems.

Based on their collective industry experience, the team identified many "quick hits" which they believed could turn the operation around, so they opted for an acquisition, rather than to risk starting from scratch.

As a result of vastly improved quality and service, the operation quickly changed from 1 shift 5 days per week to 3 shifts 7 days per week, which put huge demands on hiring employees, as well as creating a need for additional capital for new machines.

Don Smith quickly employed his extensive industrial blow molding experience to improve productivity and quality, Rona was able to hire more than 100 employees, mostly from the local vocational school, and Paul spent most of his time that first year with bankers and private placement investors, to fund the growth.

Early in the third year and after placing a strong emphasis on quality and service, **Fremont Plastics** became one of the first industrial blow molders to acquire the coveted Q1 rating from Ford, which opened the door to bidding opportunities on new business.

Also, as **Fremont's** industry reputation grew, they were able to expand their business with Little Tikes and they acquired a number of new customers, including 3M, American Cyanamid, and Hancor Tile. Along the way, Rubbermaid acquired Little Tikes which led to even more opportunities for Fremont's other businesses.

During the ensuing years, **Fremont** continued to grow and eventually became recognized as one of the top 10 industrial blow molders in the United States. At the end of 1997, **Fremont** had more than 300 employees and sales of more than $30 million.

As **Fremont's** success continued, it was inevitable that **Fremont** would become an acquisition target and, in 1998 the Plastics Group knocked on the door. Although Paul and Rona were not actively seeking to sell the business, the need for capital to fund further growth, combined with having a highly leveraged balance sheet, caused Paul and Rona to eventually decide, in the words of a famous folk singer, "know when to hold 'em, when to fold 'em and when to walk away and when to run," to accept an offer in the spring of 1998.

It is also worth noting that during his 15 years as the owner of **Fremont Plastics, Inc.,** Paul was also a leader in helping to define industry strategies, and in 1989 he was recognized as one of first five Ernst & Young Northwest Ohio Entrepreneurs of the Year, along with myself, Peter Silverman of Shumaker Loop & Kendrick, Fritz Rudolph of Rudolph/Libbe, and Joe Links, who had founded Software Alternatives.

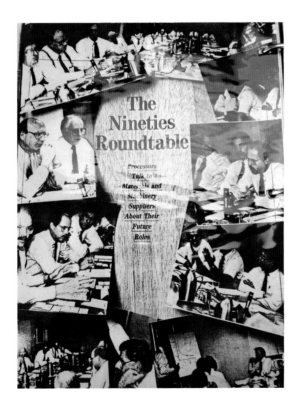

The Sponseller Group
Founder - Harold Sponseller
Former O-I Senior Designer

Harold Sponseller

Sponseller Group, Inc. is a multi-disciplined engineering firm in the Toledo area with a company goal of "To provide quality engineering services, and to offer our employees a place where they can learn and grow."

Sponseller Group, Inc. offers a broad range of personnel including professional engineers (PE's), graduate engineers, senior designers, and mechanical designers. Employees are assisted with their education and advancement through a tuition reimbursement program. All staff are encouraged in their professional careers, personal achievements, and community involvement.

The company was started by Harold Sponseller P.E., a mechanical engineer who was employed at **Owens-Illinois**. Originally, he offered mechanical engineering services through people working at his office. Later companies requested personnel to perform design services at their location. After thirteen years he began offering structural engineering and process piping services.

These areas have become the largest service offerings within the company. Most of the project work is completed at one of three offices. Additionally, **Sponseller** partners with design/build contractors and fabricators, providing them engineering and design services. Over eighty percent of **Sponseller's** projects come from existing clients.

The company's success results from consistently providing competent, quality engineering services to its clients so they will return for additional services. The members of **Sponseller** recognize that technology and the ability to implement a comprehensive support plan makes the company a trusted resource.

Sponseller's staff of engineers and designers approaches each project with the goal of taking the client from concept to completion while participating in solving any unforeseen problems that arise and they work with clients to continually upgrade operations for producing the next generation of products.

What sets **Sponseller** apart is the company's experience, attentiveness to client needs, and responsiveness. **Sponseller** employees have a long tenure since the company offers a great work environment, new computers, competitive wages and benefits and employees feel appreciated and well compensated for their level of education and engineering experience.

Harold Sponseller's son, Keith took over as president in 2008 and the company expanded to offer architectural as well as engineering services. Currently **Sponseller** has 57 full-time employees.

DuraTemp Corp
Co-Founders - Daniel Stewart with Burton Spear
Former O-I Senior R&D Managers

Dr. Daniel R. Stewart was a former Vice President of the corporate staff and Director of Glass and Ceramic Technology at **Owens-Illinois, Inc.**

Dr. Stewart retired in 1994 from **Dura Temp Corp.,** which began as one of his projects at **O-I** which was focused on how to handle hot glass and which he and Burton Spear acquired from **O-I. DuraTemp Corp.** is now owned by Dr. Stewart's son-in-law, Brian Summerson.

Before taking on **Dura Temp** in 1983, Dr. Stewart was with **O-I** for 19 years, beginning in 1964 after he received his doctorate in glass and ceramic engineering from Penn State University, where he had also received his bachelor's and master's degrees.

He became head of **O-I's Glass Science Laboratory** in 1967 and became Director of Glass and Ceramic Research in 1970. He was appointed Director of **O-I's Corporate Research Laboratories** in 1972.

He was honored as the nation's "Outstanding Young Ceramic Engineer" in 1974 by the National Institute of Ceramic Engineering. He was a former chairman of the glass division of the American Ceramics Society and U.S. representative to the International Commission on Glass.

"Dan to me was an excellent friend who stood by you and commanded respect as a professional and as an individual," said Richard Redwine, who retired in 1997 as vice president of manufacturing and engineering at Kimble Glass, formerly an **O-I** division.

"I think he had the respect of everybody who worked with him. He was straightforward and dedicated to what he was doing."

Dr. Stewart's success, his son said, was "a matter of perseverance and talent. He was a technical expert in his field and was capable of talking about his subject."

Dr. Stewart was a former assistant Boy Scout leader and volunteered with the Church of the Nazarene, of which he was a former board member and treasurer, his son said.

Dr. Stewart was born in New Kensington, Pa., and was president of his graduating class at Arnold, Pa., High School.

Franklin Electric
CEO – Scott Trumbull
Former O-I Senior Vice President

Scott and Margy Trumbull

After earning his bachelor's degree at Denison University and his MBA at Harvard, Scott Trumbull joined Owens-Illinois, Inc. where he moved up quickly to become Executive Vice President and Chief Financial Officer. At O-I he oversaw international operations, including O-I's acquisition of formerly state-run glass facilities in Eastern Europe after the fall of the communist regimes.

Scott first joined the **Franklin Electric, Inc.** board in 1998 and left O-I in 2002 to become Chairman and Chief Executive Officer. During his tenure, **Franklin Electric, Inc.** transformed itself from being a submersible motor supplier for pump manufacturers to being a pumping systems supplier for distributors.

Additionally, the company's revenues grew to $965 million in 2013 with 37 percent of those revenues coming from developing region international markets. Under Mr. Trumbull's leadership, the company's market capitalization increased from $520 million to $1.9 billion.

Scott and Margy Trumbull with sons, Matt, Ben and Will

Franklin Electric, Inc. remains a global leader in the production and marketing of systems and components for the movement of water and automotive fuels. Recognized as a technical leader in its specialties, **Franklin Electric, Inc.** serves customers around the world in residential, commercial, agricultural, industrial, municipal, and fueling applications. Scott retired from **Franklin Electric, Inc**. in 2015.

Scott also served as a director of Welltower Inc., Calphalon Company, Schneider National, Artisan Partners Fund, Columbus McKinnon, Inc., ProMedica, and the Toledo Museum of Art. He served as a life trustee at Denison University.

Imaging Systems Technology (ITS)/formerly Digivue
Founders - Don Wedding, Carol Wedding
Former O-I Patent Attorney and his daughter

Website: https://www.trelleborg.com/en/applied-technologies

Imaging Systems Technologies (IST) developed as a small privately held materials and electronics firm located in Toledo, Ohio. **IST** is engaged in research and development of large area distributed electronic networks including flexible displays and flexible sensors. **IST** provides electronic development and consulting with focus in displays, imaging, and optical technology. Display technology includes AC plasma, DC plasma, LCD, and EL and their related drive electronics. Imaging Technology includes high-speed video signal processing, high-speed digital signal processing, and image enhancement. Optical technology includes custom and stock telecentric and field splitting lenses. Additionally, **IST** has proficiency in embedded micro control, signal capture and analysis. **IST** manufactures several electronic products including a line of large area touch screens for tele-stration, wayfinding, and kiosks. The **IST** team includes scientists, engineers, and technicians from various backgrounds with various degrees including doctorates, masters, and Bachelor of Science.

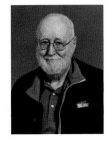  **IST** was founded in 1997 by the University of Toledo professor, Don Wedding, and his daughter and co-founder Carol Wedding who is now President of **IST**. She is an electrical engineer with over 25 years of experience in display electronics and prior to assuming the presidency, Ms. Wedding managed business development for **IST**, oversaw IP development, and assisted with project management.

IST was recently acquired by Trelleborg Applied Technologies, headquartered in Norway, with offices around the world. Trelleborg delivers innovative and reliable solutions that maximize performance for a vast range of specialized, customizable materials and offers customers reliable and efficient project management and manufacturing by taking performance to new levels by achieving its customers' goals safely, on time and within scope.

Trelleborg Applied Technologies can trace its roots all the way back to 1905 when Henry Dunker founded Trelleborg Gummifabriks AB and turned it into Scandinavia's leading rubber production company. The inception of Trelleborg Applied Technologies in 2016 followed a 20-year period of market consolidation of well-known brands such as Advanced Engineering Materials, Ambler Technologies, Emerson and Cuming, CRP, OCP, Tyco, Polyurethane Products Limited and Unitex. Today, Trelleborg Applied Technologies continues to be a world-leader of specialized, customizable material solutions.

Helm Instruments
Founder - Don Wilhelm
Former O-I Instrumentation Manager

Website: https://www.helminstrument.com

Helm instruments was founded by Don Wilhelm in 1962. **Helm Instruments** recently announced Mike Wilhelm as the new President of **Helm Instrument Company**. Mike has been a dedicated member of the Helm team for the past 44 years.

50-year Helm Instrument anniversary speech
By Rick Wilhelm

"Twenty years from now you will be more disappointed by the things you didn't do than the ones you did do. So, throw off the bowlines. Sail away from the safe harbor. Catch the trade winds in your sails. Explore! Dream! Discover!"

It was 1959 when a young technician working at **Owens – Illinois** had an idea, an idea on how a newly developed technology; a device called a transistor could be used to better control the temperature of the company's glass and plastic molding furnaces.

The idea became a quest for him, and the quest soon turned into a passion. Unfortunately, his colleagues eschewed the concept of this thermocouple-based instrument, and corporate funding was not provided. Un-deterred, he set out to develop the unit in the basement of his home. After three years of many attempts and failures the final design was complete and needed only field testing. The instrument, which was a digital set-point temperature controller, would be called the **Helmsman,** and in 1961 the first installation of a **Helmsman** was completed at the Owens facility in Alton IL. That first installation was only the beginning... There would be many more ideas, and many more quests to pursue, and each would be taken on with the same unwavering commitment and burning passion.   You see the real **Helmsman** was not the instrument it was Donald Wilhelm who named this fledgling company **Helm Instrument** and had the company incorporated in the State of Ohio in 1962.

The journey had thus begun. The bowlines had been cast from the pier and **Helm** would set course on a long journey; a journey that has now entered in to its 50th year. It was a motley crew at the time. There were no graduate engineers or PHD's on board, it was just handfuls of dedicated and hard-working men and women, who believed, and were willing to take the risk

In almost all cases the journey would take the crew into uncharted waters. It was certainly not an easy journey, as many times it would encounter strong headwinds and enter into troubled seas.

But the **Helmsman**, he never lost his vision. Encouraged by his wife, Nancy, and knowing that his direction was being guided by the Lord, he steered the ship with innate confidence. There was no compass or sexton on board: he never felt they were needed... And his steadfast confidence….. Oh, how he instilled in his crew, which now is in its third generation with graduate engineers from universities such as Notre Dame, Michigan State, Michigan, Bowling Green and Toledo to name just a few. And when faced with adversity and seemingly certain failure, when the ship was taking on way too much water, the **Helmsman,** he would simply put it on "auto-pilot" and go around the ship reminding the crew that that this storm would pass, and they were all up to the challenge and capable of doing more and that it was incumbent upon them to think big. Think global. Think export.

The **Helmsman** would never let the ship set anchor for long. And when it did it was only to add more crew members, plot a new more challenging course and catch the trade winds. Along the way it would continue to develop new products for new applications using the latest technology to provide industry with innovative process control solutions.

In 1965 the company would chart a new and certainly more venturesome course, as the **Helmsman** recognized an opportunity to develop a product that would measure and control force instead of temperature.

That change in course would lead the way for **Helm Instrument** to become the recognized industry leader in the field force measurement technology used on production machines. Over the years, Don received numerous patents for his designs in the areas of sensors and instrumentation.

Helm became part of a strong armada as it entered into a long-standing relationship with Rockwell Automation in 1991. As a Global Encompass partner Helm has integrated its force measurement technology into the various Allen-Bradley PLC platforms in the form of plug-in modules.

Through this partnership the application of **Helm** force measurement technology has expanded into many new markets, many new industries with countless new applications. Today, **Helm** force monitors are used to control a wide array of processes including, packing, weighing, filling and printing, and in industries such as petrochemical, pharmaceutical, automotive, food and beverage, electronics, avionics, and the military.

Strong trade winds moved the ship to the shores across Europe as **Helm e**stablished agencies in the U.K, Germany, Spain, Italy, the Netherlands, France, Poland and the Czech Republic... Other agents were established in Canada and Mexico. The success in Europe led to the hiring of European operations Mgr. based in the U.K in 1998.

Exports expanded to the Asian market starting in 2000 with agencies being appointed in Japan, China, South Korea, Taiwan, Singapore, Hong Kong, Malaysia, Indonesia and India.

The **Helmsman** passed away in December of 2006, just a year before his company received the highly prestige's Governor's Excellence in export award from the State of Ohio. Today, over 60% of the company's sales are export through a global network of agencies in almost every continent.

Through the guidance of Don Wilhelm, and with his tutelage, today his sons, daughters, grandchildren and spirited crew working for Helm have a clear vision for the future, and that vision is to continue to provide industry with innovative technology based on the standards of integrity and quality, with a firm belief our standards will be upheld by promoting the individual standards of excellence from our dedicated and spirited crewmembers. While never veering off course we must plan for and respond to the needs of our changing world.

Trusting in the Lord, and with integrity and quality as our guide, we are led to new destinations with clear objectives, confident leadership and commitment by all. We will use the momentum, the memories and the lessons of the past half century to guide us through the next adventure.

It is my deepest privilege and honor to serve as President and be at the **Helm** as we celebrate our 50th anniversary; but, I know, as we all do, that there will only ever be one, true, **Helmsman**.

May God bless you all; and may God continue to Bless **Helm Instrument**.

Contributed by Mike and Rick Wilhelm

Techni-Plex
CEO - Paul Young
Former O-I Senior Engineering Associate

Website: https://tekni-plex.com/about/

Alex, Paul, Pam, and Andrew Young

I started as an intern with **O-I** while attending the University of Toledo and while studying Chemical Engineering. During my internships at **O-I**, I worked closely with Gary Hager in the development lab and with John Kilbane, Scott Steele, Bob Deardurff, Jane Kerr, and many other great **O-I** engineers. Whether it was dropping 3-liter CSD bottles out the window for drop test results or measuring preform finish dimensions, I loved the work and, more importantly, the people. There were no more talented people in the industry at that time than Andy Dickson, Jim Fargher, and Frank Semersky, and I loved learning from them.

When I graduated from UT, I interviewed with Tom Brady who to me was the "Godfather of **O-I** Plastics," and I was lucky enough to be hired permanently. As a new employee, I first worked for Scott Steele starting up new blow molds and new blow molding machines in the four **O-I Plastic Beverage Operations (PBO)** plants in Fairfield, CA, where we started up 3 and 4-liter wine bottles on Krupp BAB-4 machines, and in Havre de Grace, MD, where I worked with people like Skip Wood starting up oval BBQ bottles, and in Milford, CT and Dallas, TX where we started up the first 3-liter soft drink bottle production.

I loved learning as much as I could from all the people on the team and I will never forget the importance of working with small teams of engineers, pushing the technology, understanding the mathematical nature of plastics, and learning about extension ratios and the importance of orientation, and best of all, having the chance to work with and learn from great management.

Perhaps my most vivid memory of those early years was marveling at the mathematical capabilities of Dr. Long Fei Chang who created the algorithms that provided the theoretical background for oriented PET bottle technology, and which ultimately proved to be **O-I's** competitive advantage.

I also worked with John Matuszak helping to teach the Campbell Soup Company how to fabricate the world's first crystallized PET (CPET) trays for frozen dinner foods and which quickly replaced the original aluminum foil trays.

I left **O-I** just as PET for carbonated soft drink packaging became commoditized in the mid-late 80's and I joined **Continental Plastic Ventures**, a division of the **Continental Can Company**. **Continental** was worried about plastics eating into their metal can food business, but I had the opportunity to transfer the MenuBox technology which came to **Continental** from Belgium and Switzerland, and I had responsibility for starting up an entire plant in West Chicago, IL where we extruded multilayer polypropylene (PP) sheet for thermoforming shelf-stable retortable food packaging, and where we also produced multilayer polystyrene (PS) sheet for aseptic food packaging using Erca FFS machines.

Another division of the **Continental Can Company, Continental PET Technologies (CPT),** was run by Jerry Kerins and was building plants to convert glass beer, ketchup, and juice containers to PET using **Continental's** proprietary multiplayer and heat set (hot fill) technologies.

I started up the Hazleton, PA plant in 1992, and ran the plant as plant manager until 1996 when I was promoted to become Manufacturing Manager, reporting to George Erwin, with responsibility for building plants in Sorocaba, Brazil for Gatorade, and for Coca-Cola in Jacarepagua (Rio de Janeiro).

Continental PET Technologies (CPT) was then sold to **O-I** in 1998 after **Continental PET Technologies** had developed a barrier PET beer bottle for Miller Brewing Co., and, in part, because **O-I** was worried about its glass beer and tea (Snapple) franchises converting to PET. Joe Lemieux was CEO of **O-I** at that time and Russ Berkoben was General Manager of the **Plastic Products Division**. I reported to Mike McDaniel, **Plastic Products Division** Manufacturing Manager, and I had responsibility for the 9 (formerly) **CPT** manufacturing plants.

However, even though **O-I** now owned the **CPT** proprietary PET technologies, the entire PET bottle manufacturing business across the US rapidly became commoditized, as Pepsi bought Gatorade and leveraged their size to force suppliers like **O-I** to lower prices.

In 2004 and soon after purchasing the **CPT** PET business, **O-I** decided to sell their entire **Plastic Products Division**, including the recently acquired **CPT** technologies and businesses, to **Graham Packaging**.

As a young but new **Graham Packaging** executive, I was given the opportunity to manage the integration of **O-I's** plastic bottle business (then $1B in sales) into **Graham Packaging's** plastic bottle business, which we estimated delivered $90M in synergies. After that assignment, I worked for Ashok Sudan as General Manager of the entire **Graham Packaging** PET bottle business, then a $900M business with 25 plants.

However, I left **Graham** in 2007 when my wife was diagnosed with breast cancer, and I joined **Oaktree Capital** in LA where Jerry Kerins and I were responsible for handling the due diligence on **Oaktree's** packaging business acquisitions. After just 6 months I accepted the CEO role with **Tekni-Plex** which **Oaktree** acquired in June of 2008.

I will retire from **Tekni-Plex** in June 2021 after managing what has been a fun and successful business turnaround, and after overseeing 15 acquisitions over the intervening years to reposition **Tekni-Plex** as a specialty healthcare, dispensing, and food packaging business, nearly quadrupling the profits.

It was all fun, and it started with **Owens-Illinois** and Tom Brady. Thank you, Tom!

Contributed by Paul Young